Wild Flower Walks

in Dorset

Peter & Margaret Cramb

P. & M. Cramb

First published in 2006
by P. & M. Cramb
32 Pitchers, Salway Ash,
Bridport, Dorset DT6 5QS

Maps based on Ordnance Survey mapping
under Licence No. 100044737.

ISBN 0 9537746 2 7

British Library Cataloguing-in-Publication Data.
A catalogue record for this book is
available from the British Library.

Printed by Henry Ling Limited,
The Dorset Press, Dorchester DT1 1HD

CONTENTS

Cover photographs
Front: Red Valerian on Portland
Back: Bee Orchids

ACKNOWLEDGEMENTS

We are most grateful to the following for permission to reproduce copyright material in this book:

John Fowles *John Fowles The Journals: Volume 1* (edited by Charles Drazin), Jonathan Cape 2003.
> Reproduced with the permission of Gillon Aitken Associates Ltd.

P.D. James *The Black Tower*, Sphere Books 1977.
> Reproduced with the permission of the author.

H.J. Massingham *The English Downland*, Batsford 1936.
> Reproduced with the permission of The Society of Authors as the Literary Representative of the Estate of H.J. Massingham.

Llewelyn Powys *Dorset Essays*, Redcliffe Press Ltd. 1983.
> Reproduced with the permission of Sally Connely.

Sylvia Townsend Warner *The Diaries of Sylvia Townsend Warner* (edited by Claire Harman), Chatto & Windus 1994.
> Reproduced with the permission of Susanna Pinney.

Andrew Young *A Prospect of Flowers*, Jonathan Cape 1945, and *The Bee-Orchis* from *The Collected Poems of Andrew Young*, Rupert Hart-Davis 1960.
> Reproduced with the permission of Ruth Lowbury.

Andrew Young *A Prehistoric Camp* and *The Slow Race* from *Andrew Young Selected Poems* (edited by Edward Lowbury and Alison Young), Carcanet Press Limited 1998.
> Reproduced with the permission of the publishers.

We are also grateful to the Countryside Agency for permission to use the text of the Countryside Code.

We should also like to thank Rosemary Goad and Morine Krissdóttir for their kind assistance, and Lissy Heathershaw, Dave Ackerley and Steve Kourik of Dorset County Council for their help in clarifying rights of way for some of the walks.

We believe we have obtained all necessary permissions to reproduce copyright material used in this book: should this not be the case we offer our apologies and will ensure that due acknowledgement is made in any reprint.

INTRODUCTION

The sense of well-being which comes from walking in Dorset's unsurpassed countryside is reason enough to put on your walking boots. The walks chosen for this book, spread across the county and including many different types of landscape, have the added attraction that they are all memorable for their wild flowers.

Different landscapes support distinctive groups of wild flowers, reflecting the conditions in which they grow - for example, the flowers found on chalk downland differ from those on heathland or on the shingle of the Chesil Bank. As a result, you can expect to see a great variety of flowers as you try the different walks.

For each walk we have suggested a time of year when the flowers mentioned are usually at their best, although you should still find the walks enjoyable at other times.

Dorset's beautiful landscape and wild flowers have inspired successive generations of writers and we have included some of their most evocative pieces to enhance our own words, paintings and photographs. Dorset has an outstanding richness of wild flowers, landscape and literature: we hope that this book will add to your enjoyment of them all.

Opposite: Early-purple Orchid and Cowslip

CARE AND SAFETY

Safety warning

Two of the walks (2 and 7) include stretches along cliff tops and these may be subject to landslips.

In the interests of safety, please therefore **always**:

- keep strictly to the route and marked paths.
- observe any indicated diversions.
- keep well back from the cliff edges.
- take special care in poor weather conditions.

Please also see the warning at the start of the route description for Walk 8.

For all the walks we suggest you use common sense and take appropriate precautions. Always wear stout well-gripping footwear, preferably walking boots, to reduce the risk of slipping.

Rights of Way

All the routes described in this book follow rights of way or permissive paths, or go across Open Access land. Some small lanes and tracks, marked with broken orange lines on the maps, have the status of Unclassified County Roads and carry certain rights for walkers, horse riders, cyclists and motor vehicles.

You may find a compass helpful in following the directions.

Follow The Countryside Code:

- Be safe - plan ahead and follow any signs.
- Leave gates and property as you find them.
- Protect plants and animals, and take your litter home.
- Keep dogs under close control.
- Consider other people.

Walk Locations ✿

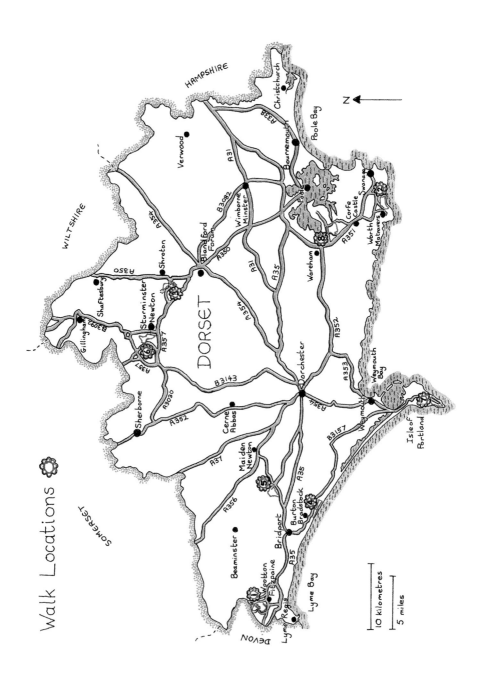

THE WALKS

WALK 1

SPRING FLOWERS IN DORSET'S FAR WEST
Coney's Castle - Wootton Fitzpaine - Wootton Hill

An early spring walk in the far west of the county. Starting at an Iron Age hill-fort, with panoramic views over the Marshwood Vale, we follow a country lane and then walk over farmland down to the attractive village of Wootton Fitzpaine.

Leaving the village by another lane we climb to the woods on Wootton Hill before making our way back to Coney's Castle over fields, lanes and tracks.

Throughout the walk we see early spring flowers, including Lesser Celandine and Wild Daffodil; both bring to mind William Wordsworth, who lived for two years with his sister Dorothy at Racedown, about three miles north-east of Coney's Castle.

Time of year:	late February to early April
Distance:	about 5 miles (8 km)
Difficulty:	fairly strenuous with some hills
Parking:	small National Trust car park off minor road at SY 372 977 (free)
Directions to car park:	going south from Marshwood on the B3165 take a left turn about 1¼ miles (2 km) past the Bottle Inn signposted "Fishponds" (ignoring an earlier sign to Fishponds). Follow this road for 1 mile (1½ km), ignoring all side turnings. The car park is on your left 700 yards (640 m) after you pass under prominent power lines.
Ordnance Survey maps:	1:50,000 Landranger 193 Taunton & Lyme Regis 1:25,000 Explorer 116 Lyme Regis & Bridport
Public transport:	76 bus to Wootton Fitzpaine from Bridport (Wednesdays only: check timetable)
Refreshments:	none (nearest in Marshwood)
Toilets:	none

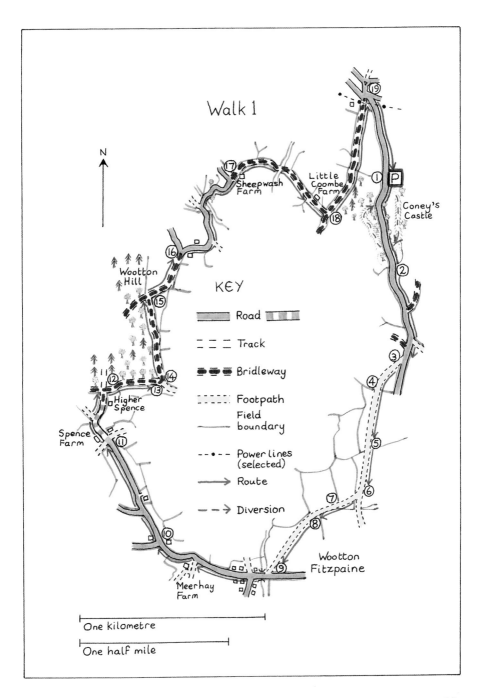

Walk 1

N

Coney's Castle

Little Coombe Farm

Sheepwash Farm

Wootton Hill

KEY

	Road	
- - -	Track	
●■●■	Bridleway	
⋯⋯	Footpath	
——	Field boundary	
- - ● - -	Power lines (selected)	
→	Route	
- -→	Diversion	

Higher Spence

Spence Farm

Wootton Fitzpaine

Meerhay Farm

One kilometre

One half mile

ROUTE

Coney's Castle

Few places seem to bring to mind more vividly the activities of our ancient ancestors than the grassy banks and deep ditches of their hill-forts, created in the Iron Age over 2,000 years ago.

Coney's Castle is one of several hill-forts in this area - others include Lambert's Castle and Pilsdon Pen. It has well-preserved ditches and banks and on a clear day the views are outstanding.

To see the hill-fort leave the car park at the National Trust information board and turn left (east) on to a footpath. Follow the footpath between the banks and round to the right (south). Armies of dark green blades have colonised the ground around you, promising the sensory onslaught of a mass of bluebells in May. Flowering now, you may see the more subtle charms of the Climbing Corydalis, with its creamy white flowers on clambering stems.

From the outer bank you have a panoramic view of the surrounding countryside: to your left (north) is Lambert's Castle, your half left (north-east) Pilsdon Pen and Lewesdon Hill, ahead of you (east) Eggardon Hill, another Iron Age hill-fort (see Walk 5) and beneath you the Marshwood Vale. Further round to your right (south-east) you will see the distant Hardy Monument, Colmer's Hill, Portland (see Walk 7), Hardown Hill and Golden Cap.

Continue around the eastern edge of the fort until you reach a stile at the road. Cross the road and walk around the western edge, with fine views down to the sea at Charmouth (south) and towards Devon (west), until you reach the car park.

1.   Turn left on leaving the car park and follow the road downhill (south).
   Ivy-leaved Speedwell, Lesser Celandine, Townhall Clock and Wood-sorrel can be seen on the verges beside the road.
   After ¼ mile (400 metres) the road emerges from trees at the south end of Coney's Castle and you see the sea beyond Charmouth, with views to your left (east) over the Marshwood Vale and to your right (west) towards Devon.
2.   Continue down the road for a further ¼ mile (400 metres).
   There are Primroses and Wild Daffodils on the verges here.
   Ignore the bridleway to your right but turn right (west) through the gate 50 yards (45 metres) further on and take the footpath waymarked "Wessex Ridgeway" and "Liberty Trail". (You will be following these waymarks until stage 9.)
3.   Walk half left (south-west) down the field; after 100 yards (90 metres) swing slightly to your left. Continue until you reach a stile after a further 100 yards (90 metres).
   There is an attractive group of Cuckooflowers to your right just before the stile.

Above: *Wild Daffodils*
Opposite: *View from Coney's Castle to the west.*

Wild Daffodil

William Wordsworth's "host of golden daffodils" can still be seen in this part of Dorset in woods, hedgerows and, sometimes, fields. Flowering from mid-February, they lift your spirits on a late winter's day.

Wild Daffodils have a more delicate appearance than most cultivated varieties. Their long, narrow, yellow trumpets are surrounded by paler, often twisted, petals.

On this walk, you will usually see these lovely flowers in small groups but, here and there, they grow in profusion. Sometimes, a shaft of sunlight and a gentle breeze enhance their beauty:

> "And then my heart with pleasure fills,
> And dances with the daffodils."
>
> William Wordsworth

4. Cross the stile into the next field; continue straight on (roughly south) for ¼ mile (400 metres) across the middle of the field to a gate close to the far right hand corner. There are good views to your right (west) as you cross the field.

5. Go through the gate and continue in the same direction (roughly south) for 220 yards (200 metres) towards the far right hand corner of the next field; 50 yards (45 metres) before reaching a gate in the corner go through a waymarked gate on your right into the next field.

6. Bear left (south-west) and walk for 100 yards (90 metres) towards the gate in the far left corner of the field.

7. Go through this gate into the next field and continue (west) along the left edge for 100 yards (90 metres), ignoring a gate after 50 yards (45 metres), until you reach a waymarked gate on your left.

8. Go through this gate into the next field; turn half right (south-west) and go down the field diagonally for 500 yards (460 metres), with Wootton Fitzpaine ahead of you, to a stile in the far right corner.

Opposite: Wild Daffodils

Lesser Celandine

"There is a Flower, the lesser Celandine,
That shrinks, like many more, from cold and rain;
And, the first moment that the sun may shine,
Bright as the sun himself, 'tis out again!"

From *The Small Celandine*,
William Wordsworth

Wordsworth's lines charmingly describe this delightful member of the Buttercup family, which is found in woodlands, hedgerows and verges throughout Dorset.

The flowers are about 1 inch (2½ cm) across with usually about 8 - but sometimes as many as 11 - shiny yellow petals surrounding a mass of yellow stamens. The long-stalked leaves are more or less heart-shaped, often with a pale mottling on their shiny dark green surfaces.

9.　　Cross the stile and turn right (west) on to the road. Cross the small bridge and continue for 100 yards (90 metres) to a junction. Continue straight ahead (roughly west) along the road signposted "Monkton Wyld" and "Fishpond".

The hedgerow along this road contains many spring flowers including Bush Vetch, Lesser Celandine, Primrose, Wild Daffodil and Yellow Archangel.

After 350 yards (320 metres) you will reach Meerhay Farm where the Wessex Ridgeway and Liberty Trail are waymarked going off to the left. Do not follow these but continue along the road (roughly north-west) for a further 250 yards (230 metres) up the hill until you reach a road junction.

Shortly after Meerhay Farm there is a very attractive bank of Cuckooflowers on your right.

10.　　Go straight ahead (roughly north) at the junction along the road signposted "Lamberts Castle" and "Forest Walks". Continue uphill for 700 yards (640 metres) to Spence Farm, ignoring a left turn (signposted "Fishponds") after 200 yards (180 metres).

11.　　Continue straight ahead (north-west) through the farmyard and remain on the track as it bears right (roughly north-east) after 100 yards (90 metres); after a further 100 yards (90 metres) pass Higher Spence on your right and continue up the track for a similar distance until you reach a wood.

Above: *Lesser Celandine*

Below: *Primrose*

12. Turn right (east) and proceed along a bridleway running close to the south edge of the wood, with splendid views on your right to the south and south-east, until you reach a gate after 350 yards (320 metres). *Townhall Clock or Moschatel is frequent around here.*

13. Go through this gate and bear left (roughly north-east); after a further few yards turn sharply left next to a gate and follow the waymarked bridleway (roughly north).

14. Walk along the east edge of the wood for ¼ mile (400 metres) until you reach a gate straight ahead of you.

15. Go through this gate, turn right (roughly north-east) and follow a bridleway along the edge of the field for 200 yards (180 metres) to the corner; turn left (roughly north) and continue along the east edge of the field for a further 200 yards (180 metres) until you reach a gate on your right, ignoring a nearer gate into a garden.

16. Go through the gate on to a road, continue straight on (roughly east) and follow the road downhill for 250 yards (230 metres) where it turns sharply left. Continue along this winding road (generally north) for 600 yards (550 metres) until it turns sharply left again at Sheepwash Farm. *Fine groups of Wild Daffodils can be seen in the fields to your left and right; pink Primroses are also sometimes found in the hedgerows around here.*

Top left: *Townhall Clock, Moschatel*
Middle left: *Cuckooflower*
Bottom left: *Yellow Archangel*
Opposite: *Wood Anemone*

17. Do not follow the road round to your left but take the bridleway straight ahead of you (north-east). After 100 yards (90 metres) go through a gate and continue along the bridleway as it curves to the right and drops to a small valley after 250 yards (230 metres) - the route can be muddy here in wet weather.

Fine clumps of Primroses and Wood Anemones are found along the bridleway. You may also see Early-purple Orchids on the left hand hedgebank here in April.

Continue on the bridleway as it rises on the other side of the valley (roughly south-east), going through a gate on the way until, after 300 yards (270 metres), you reach a further gate at Little Coombe Farm. Go through the gate with the farmhouse on your left and up the farm track for 100 yards (90 metres) until you reach a junction with another track.

18. Turn left (roughly north-east) on to this track and follow it up the hill for 700 yards (640 metres) until you reach a gate. Go through the gate, pass under power lines and continue for a few yards until you reach a road junction.

19. Turn right (roughly south) on to the road signposted "Wootton Fitzpaine". Pass under the power lines again and follow the road for 700 yards (640 metres), with fine views to both sides, until you reach Coney's Castle car park on your left.

Some of the flowers you may see on this walk

Barren Strawberry *(Potentilla sterilis)*
Bluebell *(Hyacinthoides non-scripta)*
Bush Vetch *(Vicia sepium)*
Bilberry *(Vaccinium myrtillus)*
Climbing Corydalis
  (Ceratocapnos claviculata)
Common Chickweed *(Stellaria media)*
Common Dog-violet *(Viola riviniana)*
Common Field-speedwell
  (Veronica persica)
Cow Parsley *(Anthriscus sylvestris)*
Cuckooflower *(Cardamine pratensis)*
Dandelions *(Taraxacum agg.)*
Dog's Mercury *(Mercurialis perennis)*
Early-purple Orchid *(Orchis mascula)*
Field Pansy *(Viola arvensis)*
Germander Speedwell
  (Veronica chamaedrys)
Gorse *(Ulex europaeus)*
Greater Stitchwort *(Stellaria holostea)*
Ground-ivy *(Glechoma hederacea)*
Hairy Bitter-cress *(Cardamine hirsuta)*
Ivy-leaved Speedwell
  (Veronica hederifolia)

Ivy-leaved Toadflax
  (Cymbalaria muralis)
Lesser Celandine *(Ranunculus ficaria)*
Opposite-leaved Golden-saxifrage
  (Chrysosplenium oppositifolium)
Primrose *(Primula vulgaris)*
Red Campion *(Silene dioica)*
Red Dead-nettle *(Lamium purpureum)*
Scentless Mayweed
  (Tripleurospermum inodorum)
Snowdrop *(Galanthus nivalis)*
Townhall Clock, Moschatel
  (Adoxa moschatellina)
White Dead-nettle *(Lamium album)*
Wild Daffodil
  (Narcissus pseudonarcissus)
Wild Strawberry *(Fragaria vesca)*
Wood Anemone *(Anemone nemorosa)*
Wood-sorrel *(Oxalis acetosella)*
Yellow Archangel
  (Lamiastrum galeobdolon)

Opposite: View from Coney's Castle to the south-east.

WALK 2

EARLY SPIDER-ORCHIDS ALONG THE PURBECK COAST
Worth Matravers, Winspit and Dancing Ledge

A spring walk along the Purbeck coast. Starting at the attractive Purbeck stone village of Worth Matravers we walk over farmland and along a track to reach the sea at Winspit where there is an abandoned limestone quarry.

We then join the coast path and follow it eastwards along cliffs and past more old quarries until we reach Dancing Ledge. Along this section there are fine views of the South Purbeck coast.

From here we climb inland over fields to the Priest's Way, an old track created in the Middle Ages to link Worth Matravers with the then smaller Swanage. We follow the track and then, after a short walk over farmland and along roads, return to our starting point.

We see many spring flowers of the coast, including the rare Early Spider-orchid, breathtakingly abundant in a good season, and, on the cliffs, Wild Cabbage.

Time of year:	mid-April to mid-May
Distance:	about 5 miles (8 km)
Difficulty:	moderately strenuous with some steep sections
Parking:	car park off minor road at SY 974 777 (small charge - honesty box)
Directions to car park:	from the A351 at the south end of Corfe Castle take the B3069 signposted "Kingston 1 Worth Matravers 3"; go through Kingston and after 1 mile (1½ km) take the first turn on the right signposted "Worth Matravers". Continue along this road for 1 mile (1½ km) until you reach the car park on your right on the outskirts of the village.
Ordnance Survey maps:	1:50,000 Landranger 195 Bournemouth & Purbeck 1:25,000 Explorer OL15 Purbeck & South Dorset
Public transport:	144 bus to Worth Matravers from Swanage (check timetable)
Refreshments:	in Worth Matravers
Toilets:	at car park

Walk 2

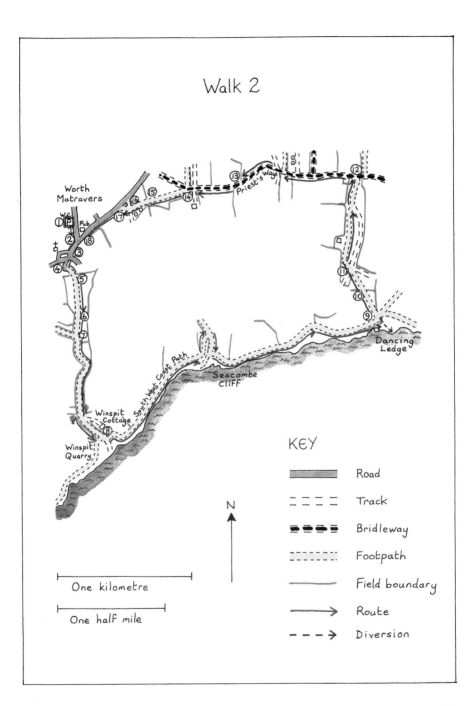

KEY

▬▬▬	Road
– – – –	Track
▰▰▰▰	Bridleway
⋯⋯⋯	Footpath
───	Field boundary
──→	Route
– – →	Diversion

One kilometre

One half mile

N

ROUTE

1. Turn right (south) on leaving the car park and follow the road downhill for 150 yards (135 metres) until you reach a junction.
2. Bear right (south-west) at the junction and after 75 yards (70 metres) take the road to your left (roughly south).
3. Follow this road, passing a road to your left and with a memorial garden on your right; after 50 yards (45 metres) take a road to your left (roughly south-west).
4. After 50 yards (45 metres) take a footpath slightly to your left (roughly south-east) and continue for a further 75 yards (70 metres) until you reach a gate.
5. Go through the gate into a field from where you will see the sea; there are strip lynchets (long narrow terraces resulting from medieval agriculture) on the slopes ahead of you. Follow the footpath down the field (roughly south) for 350 yards (320 metres) until you reach a gate.
6. Go through the gate and continue (south) on the footpath with bushes on your left and a fence on your right until after 200 yards (180 metres) you reach a junction with a track.
7. Turn left (roughly south-east) on to the track and follow it (generally south) for about ½ mile (800 metres) until you reach the coast path at Winspit Quarry.
   Crosswort can be found part way along this track on your right.

Early Gentian

This lovely flower is found only in Britain, with Dorset one of its strongholds.

It grows in short turf on chalk and limestone and there is a good population in the Dancing Ledge area. The plant is an annual or biennial and the numbers vary from year to year.

The mauvish-purple flowers are shaped like an up-turned bell with 4 or 5 pointed petal lobes around a fringed centre. The leaves are narrow and pointed, growing in opposite pairs.

It can be difficult to find, both because the flowers are usually only open in bright weather and because of the plant's small size - sometimes less than 2 inches (5 cm) tall.

8.　Turn left (roughly north-east) on to the coast path and follow it (generally north-east) for about 1½ miles (2½ km) until you reach a wall shortly before a National Trust sign for Dancing Ledge on your right. There are good views ahead of you along the coast towards Durlston.
Many spring flowers can be found along here including Chalk Milkwort, Early Forget-me-not, Early Gentian, Early Spider- and Green-winged Orchids, Sea Campion, Thrift and Wild Cabbage.

There are also bluebells and gorse:
"The gorse was in bloom and the bluebells were fully out by the side of the track. Gold and blue, blue and gold. The sun was golden, the sky was blue; the sun was golden, the sea was blue."

From *Dorset Essays*, Llewelyn Powys

Above: *Early Gentian*
Opposite: *The coast path from Winspit Quarry towards Dancing Ledge.*

27

Right: Early Forget-me-not

Opposite: Green-winged Orchid

Below: Wild Cabbage beside the coast path.

Early Forget-me-not

"In the early summer, when there are forget-me-nots in the turf by the cliff's edge, minute as the bright chips of enamel in a brooch..."

From *Dorset Essays*,
Llewelyn Powys

It is surely the tiny Early Forget-me-not - found on our walk along the cliffs between Winspit and Dancing Ledge - which Llewelyn Powys is describing here.

Sometimes only 2 inches (5cm) tall, it is found in Dorset in bare places or short turf on chalk, limestone or sandy soils.

The flowers are a brilliant blue and measure less than 1/10 inch (2mm) across; the five tiny petals have white bases and surround a yellow centre. The leaves are pale green, often tinged reddish and very hairy.

Easily overlooked, it is a great joy to find one plant and then more and more as your eyes tune in to their exquisite tiny flowers!

Dancing Ledge

If you are agile you may like to make your way down to the old quarry at Dancing Ledge.

From stage 8 of the route cross one of the stiles to your right just past the wall. Go carefully down the rough steps between the rocks to the flat area below. Here you can see beneath you an old swimming pool blasted out of the rocks for a school in Langton Matravers. Enid Blyton took regular holidays in Swanage and this may have been the inspiration for a pool in one of her books.

You will see many clumps of Danish Scurvy Grass and Thrift growing on the rocks and perhaps, if you are lucky, the squat, cheering form of a puffin flying rapidly past.

9. Turn left (roughly north-west) just before the wall and follow the footpath (indicated "Langton 1¼" on the end of the wall) uphill for 250 yards (230 metres) until you reach a stile.
10. Go straight ahead at the stile and continue up the footpath (generally north-west) for 200 yards (180 metres) through an area of scrub until you reach a kissing gate ahead of you.
    Attractive carpets of Ground-ivy grow beside the path here.
11. Go through the kissing gate into a field and straight ahead (roughly north-west) across the field for 100 yards (90 metres) until you reach a hedge on the other side. [N.B. The right of way here is difficult to follow as it is customary for walkers to follow a track to the left of the wall running uphill from the gate where you entered the field.] Turn right (roughly north) and continue straight ahead uphill for 220 yards (200 metres) until you reach a track at the corner of a wall. Continue straight ahead (north) along the track (at first close to the wall on your left and then joining another track from the right) for 500 yards (460 metres) until you reach a gate.
    There is an excellent view of Swanage and the Isle of Wight to the right (roughly north-east) here.
12. Go through the gate and turn left (west) on to a track: this is the "Priest's Way". Follow this track for just over ½ mile (1 km) until you reach a stile by a gate. From here St. Aldhelm's Chapel can be seen to the half left (south-west).

Opposite: Dancing Ledge showing the old swimming pool.

Early Spider-orchid

Early Spider-orchid

"Walking one April day with a friend across a field near Brighton, I suddenly stopped. My friend stared at me in astonishment and said, 'Do you always stop and throw your hat in the air when you see a Dandelion?' I replied it was not a Dandelion I was looking at, but an Early Spider Orchid."

From *A Prospect of Flowers*, Andrew Young

This rare orchid can have that sort of effect on people! Dorset is its stronghold in Britain with almost all the Dorset population growing in short limestone turf along the coast between Winspit and Swanage. The numbers vary considerably from year to year and in a good season there is a breathtaking display in the fields to the west of Dancing Ledge.

The plant is usually about 4-8 inches (10-20 cm) tall with the flowers measuring some ¾ inch (2 cm) across. The reddish brown lip - the body of the spider - is velvety with a shiny violet π mark. This special flower is the logo of the Dorset Wildlife Trust.

"Spider orchids....Aloof, bizarre plants, with a rich brown lip, tinged gold and purple in sunlight, and delicate yellow-green wings."

From *John Fowles The Journals: Volume 1*

13. Cross the stile and continue (west) on the track for a further 400 yards (360 metres) until you reach another gate.

14. Go through the gate into a field and, leaving the Priest's Way, bear left (roughly west) and follow a footpath towards the far left hand corner of the field until, after 300 yards (270 metres), you reach a stile.

15. Cross the stile into the next field and continue (roughly west) on the footpath until, after 200 yards (180 metres), you reach a stile on the far side of the field.

16. Cross the stile, go across a track and a second stile and continue (roughly west) on the footpath for 75 yards (70 metres) until you reach a stile at a road.

17. Cross the stile and turn left (south-west) on to the road; follow it for 400 yards (360 metres) until you reach a junction shortly after passing the Square and Compass public house on your right.

18. Turn sharply right (north) at the junction and follow the road uphill for 150 yards (135 metres) until you reach the car park on your left.

Some of the flowers you may see on this walk

Black Medick *(Medicago lupulina)*
Bluebell *(Hyacinthoides non-scripta)*
Buck's-horn Plantain
    (Plantago coronopus)
Bulbous Buttercup
    (Ranunculus bulbosus)
Chalk Milkwort *(Polygala calcarea)*
Common Bird's-foot-trefoil, Eggs-and-
    Bacon *(Lotus corniculatus)*
Common Chickweed *(Stellaria media)*
Common Field-speedwell
    (Veronica persica)
Common Milkwort *(Polygala vulgaris)*
Common Vetch *(Vicia sativa)*
Common Whitlowgrass
    (Erophila verna)
Cow Parsley *(Anthriscus sylvestris)*
Cowslip *(Primula veris)*
Creeping Buttercup
    (Ranunculus repens)
Crosswort *(Cruciata laevipes)*
Daisy *(Bellis perennis)*
Dandelions *(Taraxacum agg.)*
Danish Scurvygrass
    (Cochlearia danica)
Dog's Mercury *(Mercurialis perennis)*
Early Forget-me-not
    (Myosotis ramosissima)
Early Gentian *(Gentianella anglica)*
Early Spider-orchid
    (Ophrys sphegodes)
Fairy Flax *(Linum catharticum)*
Field Forget-me-not
    (Myosotis arvensis)
Field Madder *(Sherardia arvensis)*
Garlic Mustard *(Alliaria petiolata)*
Germander Speedwell
    (Veronica chamaedrys)

Gorse *(Ulex europaeus)*
Green Alkanet
    (Pentaglottis sempervirens)
Green-winged Orchid *(Orchis morio)*
Ground-ivy *(Glechoma hederacea)*
Herb-Robert *(Geranium robertianum)*
Horseshoe Vetch *(Hippocrepis comosa)*
Ivy-leaved Speedwell
    (Veronica hederifolia)
Kidney Vetch *(Anthyllis vulneraria)*
Lesser Celandine *(Ranunculus ficaria)*
Lords-and-Ladies, Cuckoo-pint
    (Arum maculatum)
Primrose *(Primula vulgaris)*
Red Dead-nettle *(Lamium purpureum)*
Red Valerian *(Centranthus ruber)*
Ribwort Plantain *(Plantago lanceolata)*
Salad Burnet
    (Sanguisorba minor ssp. *minor)*
Scarlet Pimpernel
    (Anagallis arvensis ssp. *arvensis)*
Sea Campion *(Silene uniflora)*
Shepherd's-purse
    (Capsella bursa-pastoris)
Small-flowered Buttercup
    (Ranunculus parviflorus)
Spotted Medick *(Medicago arabica)*
Thrift, Sea Pink *(Armeria maritima)*
Thyme-leaved Speedwell
    (Veronica serpyllifolia)
Wall Speedwell *(Veronica arvensis)*
White Dead-nettle *(Lamium album)*
Wild Cabbage, Sea Cabbage
    (Brassica oleracea var. *oleracea)*
Wild Clary *(Salvia verbenaca)*
Wood Avens, Herb Bennet
    (Geum urbanum)

Opposite: *Early Spider-orchid*

WALK 3

COWSLIPS AND EARLY-PURPLE ORCHIDS ON IRON AGE HILL-FORTS
Hambledon and Hod Hills

A late spring walk on chalk downland in North Dorset. Starting at the foot of one Iron Age hill-fort, Hod Hill, we climb through farmland to another, Hambledon Hill.

We walk round its dramatic banks and ditches with panoramic views over the Blackmore Vale - Thomas Hardy's "Vale of the Little Dairies" and the early home of the Dorset poet William Barnes. We then descend over fields almost to the village of Iwerne Courtney (or Shroton).

From there we pass along woodland edges and over more fields before ascending Hod Hill. We cross the centre of the hill-fort and pass a Roman fort before finally descending to our starting point.

We see late spring flowers throughout, including Early-purple Orchids and spectacular carpets of Cowslips on Hambledon and Hod Hills.

Time of year:	late April to mid-May
Distance:	about 5½ miles (9 km)
Difficulty:	fairly strenuous with some steep hills
Parking:	small National Trust car park off minor road at ST 853 112 (free)
Directions to car park:	from the A350 take the road 1¼ miles (2 km) north of Stourpaine signposted "Hanford 1 Child Okeford 2": follow this road until you reach the car park on your left after ½ mile (¾ km).
Ordnance Survey maps:	1:50,000 Landranger 194 Dorchester & Weymouth 1:25,000 Explorer 118 Shaftesbury & Cranborne Chase
Public transport:	182, 183 buses to Iwerne Courtney ("Shroton" in timetable) from Blandford (check timetable)
Refreshments:	In Iwerne Courtney
Toilets:	None

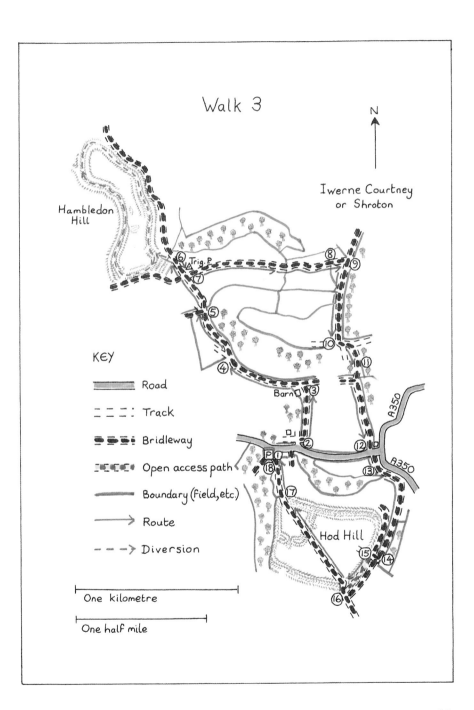

Walk 3

N

Iwerne Courtney
or Shroton

Hambledon
Hill

Trig. P

KEY

Road

Track

Bridleway

Open access path

Boundary (field, etc.)

Route

Diversion

Barn

A350

A350

Hod Hill

One kilometre

One half mile

ROUTE

1. From the car park turn right (east) along the road, taking great care of the traffic. Continue for 250 yards (230 metres) until you reach a gate on the left-hand side of the road with a sign for a bridleway (waymarked "The Stour Valley Way", which you will be following until stage 5).

2. Go through the gate into a field, turn left (north) and follow the bridleway uphill along the left (west) edge of the field for 400 yards (360 metres) until you reach a gate in the top left-hand corner shortly after a barn. As you climb the hill there are fine views of Hod Hill behind you (south). *Cow Parsley, Field Madder, Garlic Mustard, Lords-and-Ladies and Common Field-, Ivy-leaved and Thyme-leaved Speedwells are some of the flowers found along the edge of the field.*

3. Turn left (west) through the waymarked gate and continue west and then north-west on the bridleway along the right (north) edge of the field for 600 yards (550 metres) until you reach a gate.

4. Go through the waymarked gate into the next field and, bearing right (roughly north), follow the bridleway along the right edge of the field towards a wood (do not take the track across the centre of the field). Continue on the bridleway until you reach a small gate after 350 yards (320 metres).

5. Go through the gate (waymarked "Wessex Ridgeway"), not over the stile to its left (waymarked "The Stour Valley Way" and leading to the site of a Neolithic camp). Continue on the bridleway (north then north-west) for 450 yards (410 metres), passing an Ordnance Survey triangulation pillar on your right, until you reach a gate close to an English Nature sign at the entrance to Hambledon Hill.

Opposite: Early-purple Orchid on Hambledon Hill.

Hambledon Hill

"By yonder ash, above our track,
You see high Hambledon's blue back,
With rings cast up in olden time
Too steep, in hope, for foes to climb;"

From *Land Views*, William Barnes

Hambledon Hill is an outstanding example of an Iron Age hill-fort with a spectacular system of banks and ditches and magnificent views in all directions.

Start at the gate (stage 5 of the route) and walk clockwise round the fort. There are paths at different levels but if you choose the lower ones you will walk much further than if you keep to the higher ground!

From the western side of the hill you will see glimpses of the River Stour, the town of Sturminster Newton (see Walk 6) and the Blackmore Vale.

Returning along the top of the hill will take you past a well-preserved Neolithic long barrow; from here there are good views of Cranborne Chase to the north-east. Complete your tour by returning to the gate at which you started.

On and around the banks - especially on the south and west sides - is a profusion of wild flowers, surviving because the soil has escaped ploughing and the application of fertilisers and weedkillers. They include Chalk Milkwort, Cowslip (sometimes in great numbers), Early-purple Orchid, Early Gentian, Fairy Flax, Horseshoe Vetch, Hound's-tongue and Salad Burnet, while near the top are scattered groups of Meadow Saxifrage. The hill is a National Nature Reserve reflecting its importance for wildlife.

6.   Leave Hambledon Hill by the gate through which you entered and continue (south-east) for 150 yards (135 metres) until you reach the triangulation pillar.

7.   Just past the pillar turn left (east) on to another bridleway (waymarked "Wessex Ridgeway") and follow this downhill for just over ½ mile (800 metres), crossing two fields, until you reach a gate towards the bottom. As you descend the hill you will see the village of Iwerne Courtney, also called Shroton, to your half left (roughly north-east) and Ranston (house) slightly to your right (roughly east).

8.   Go through the gate into the next field and continue to follow the bridleway (east) downhill for 75 yards (70 metres) until you reach a wall.

Above: *Salad Burnet*
Opposite: *View over Blackmore Vale from Hambledon Hill*

> "The atmosphere beneath is languorous, and is so tinged
> with azure that what artists call the middle distance partakes
> also of that hue..."
> From *Tess of the d'Urbervilles*, Thomas Hardy

Cowslip

"An' cowslips up in yollow beds
Do hang their heads on downy stalks;"
From *A Pleäce in Zight*, William Barnes

Quite common in Dorset grasslands, Cowslips grow in great profusion on the tops of Hambledon and Hod Hills, safe from agricultural sprays.

Each tall, upright, downy stalk is laden with a cluster of drooping pale green sepal-tubes ("calyx-tubes") from which the deep yellow petals emerge exuberantly and fragrantly. The yellowish-green leaves are strongly veined - almost wrinkled - and narrow abruptly above the base.

9. Turn right (roughly south) at the wall on to a bridleway and follow this for 550 yards (500 metres) with the wall and then a fence on your left - the route can be muddy here in wet weather - until you reach the corner of the fence.
   The sweet-smelling Woodruff is found along the fence.
10. Turn half left (south-east) and continue on the waymarked bridleway, ignoring a track straight ahead of you; after 30 yards (27 metres) turn half right (roughly south) and continue slightly uphill with a fence and trees on your left until you reach a gate after 250 yards (230 metres).
11. Go through this gate and another gate 50 yards (45 metres) further on into a field. Bear left (roughly south) and continue downhill along the left edge of the field, with a view of Hod Hill ahead of you, for 500 yards (460 metres) until you reach a gate at a road.
12. Go through the gate, cross the road and through another gate on the far side into a field. Follow a bridleway across the field (roughly south-east) until after 150 yards (135 metres) you reach a gate towards the far side.
13. Go through this gate and another after a further 25 yards (23 metres); continue to follow the bridleway (at first south-east, then curving right to the south and south-west) uphill until you reach a gate after 700 yards (640 metres).
14. Turn right (roughly west) at the gate and continue on the waymarked bridleway for a few yards until you reach a gate at the entrance to Hod Hill.

Opposite: Cowslips

Above: *Cowslips on Hod Hill*

> "With the strengthening of the sun the wide pasture on the other side of the stile provides the earliest cowslips, short of stalk at first but tall by the end of April, and visible a long way off above the bright dairy grass."
>
> From *Dorset Essays*, Llewelyn Powys

Hod Hill

Hod Hill is Dorset's largest Iron Age hill-fort by internal area, enclosing 54 acres (22 hectares).

As you cross the central area you will see in the north-west corner the remains of a fort built by the Romans after they had stormed the hill-fort in about 43 A.D.

As at Hambledon Hill, wild flowers are found in profusion, with Cowslips carpeting the central area, interspersed with the occasional Early-purple Orchid.

The hill-fort is in the care of the National Trust.

15. Go through the gate and straight on uphill for a few yards; turn left (south-west) and walk between the outer and inner banks of the hill-fort for 250 yards (230 metres) until, just before the banks turn to your right, you see a gate on your left and a bridleway crosses ahead of you. *A fine group of Common Twayblade orchids can be found to your left on the outer bank about 150 yards (135 metres) along.*

16. Turn right (roughly north) on to this bridleway and follow it, at first uphill, across the centre of the hill-fort (roughly north-west), until after 800 yards (730 metres) you reach a stile (waymarked "The Stour Valley Way") beside a gate beyond its north-west corner.

17. Cross the stile and continue (roughly north) on the bridleway downhill, keeping close to the wood on your left, until after 300 yards (270 metres) you reach a gate (waymarked "The Stour Valley Way").

18. Go through the gate and continue straight ahead (north-west) for 50 yards (45 metres) until you reach the car park.

Top right: *Common Twayblade*

Middle right: *Meadow Saxifrage*

Bottom right: *Ramsons*

Some of the flowers you may see on this walk

Black Medick *(Medicago lupulina)*
Bluebell *(Hyacinthoides non-scripta)*
Bulbous Buttercup
  (Ranunculus bulbosus)
Chalk Milkwort *(Polygala calcarea)*
Cleavers *(Galium aparine)*
Comfreys *(Symphytum agg.)*
Common Chickweed *(Stellaria media)*
Common Dog-violet *(Viola riviniana)*
Common Field-speedwell
  (Veronica persica)
Common Mouse-ear
  (Cerastium fontanum)
Common Sorrel *(Rumex acetosa)*
Common Twayblade *(Listera ovata)*
Cow Parsley *(Anthriscus sylvestris)*
Cowslip *(Primula veris)*
Creeping Buttercup
  (Ranunculus repens)
Cut-leaved Crane's-bill
  (Geranium dissectum)
Daisy *(Bellis perennis)*
Dandelions *(Taraxacum agg.)*
Dog's Mercury *(Mercurialis perennis)*
Dove's-foot Crane's-bill
  (Geranium molle)
Early Forget-me-not
  (Myosotis ramosissima)
Early Gentian *(Gentianella anglica)*
Early-purple Orchid *(Orchis mascula)*
Fairy Flax *(Linum catharticum)*
Field Forget-me-not
  (Myosotis arvensis)
Field Madder *(Sherardia arvensis)*
Field Pansy *(Viola arvensis)*
Garlic Mustard *(Alliaria petiolata)*
Germander Speedwell
  (Veronica chamaedrys)

Ground-ivy *(Glechoma hederacea)*
Herb-Robert *(Geranium robertianum)*
Horseshoe Vetch *(Hippocrepis comosa)*
Hound's-tongue
  (Cynoglossum officinale)
Ivy-leaved Speedwell
  (Veronica hederifolia)
Leopard's-bane
  (Doronicum pardalianches)
Lesser Celandine *(Ranunculus ficaria)*
Lords-and-Ladies, Cuckoo-pint
  (Arum maculatum)
Meadow Buttercup *(Ranunculus acris)*
Meadow Saxifrage
  (Saxifraga granulata)
Musk Thistle, Nodding Thistle
  (Carduus nutans)
Pineappleweed *(Matricaria discoidea)*
Primrose *(Primula vulgaris)*
Ramsons *(Allium ursinum)*
Red Campion *(Silene dioica)*
Red Dead-nettle *(Lamium purpureum)*
Ribwort Plantain *(Plantago lanceolata)*
Salad Burnet
  (Sanguisorba minor ssp. *minor)*
Shepherd's-purse
  (Capsella bursa-pastoris)
Silverweed *(Potentilla anserina)*
Three-nerved Sandwort
  (Moehringia trinervia)
Thyme-leaved Speedwell
  (Veronica serpyllifolia)
Wall Speedwell *(Veronica arvensis)*
White Dead-nettle *(Lamium album)*
Woodruff *(Galium odoratum)*
Yellow Archangel
  (Lamiastrum galeobdolon)

Opposite: Early-purple Orchid

WALK 4

YELLOW HORNED-POPPIES, SEA-KALE AND THRIFT ON THE CHESIL BANK
Cogden and Burton Bradstock

An early summer walk along the western end of the Chesil Bank.

Starting with views of the sea below us, we walk over grassland rich with wild flowers before descending to the landward side of the Chesil Bank. We then follow the coast path westwards along the edge of marshland before emerging on to the shingle bank itself. Along this section we have fine views west towards Golden Cap and the Devon coast.

We continue on the path along low cliffs, before descending to a sandy beach at Burton Bradstock. We then retrace our steps eastwards along the coast path with good views along the Chesil Bank towards Portland, before finally climbing back to the car park.

We see a great variety of flowers, including Bee and Pyramidal Orchids in the grassland, Southern Marsh-orchids and Yellow Irises in the marshy area and special flowers of the shingle, including Sea-kale and Yellow Horned-poppies, on the Chesil Bank.

Time of year:	mid-May to early June
Distance:	about 4 miles (6½ km)
Difficulty:	fairly easy, but with a few uphill sections
Parking:	National Trust car park off the B3157 at SY 502 886 (free)
Directions to car park:	from Burton Bradstock take the B3157 eastwards towards Weymouth; you will find the car park on your right ¾ mile (1¼ km) after leaving the village and 600 yards (550 metres) beyond the entrance to The Old Coastguard Holiday Park.
Ordnance Survey maps:	1:50,000 Landranger 194 Dorchester & Weymouth 1:25,000 Explorer OL 15 Purbeck & South Dorset
Public transport:	X53 bus between Bournemouth and Exeter stops at car park (check timetable)
Refreshments:	café behind beach at Burton Bradstock
Toilets:	behind beach at Burton Bradstock

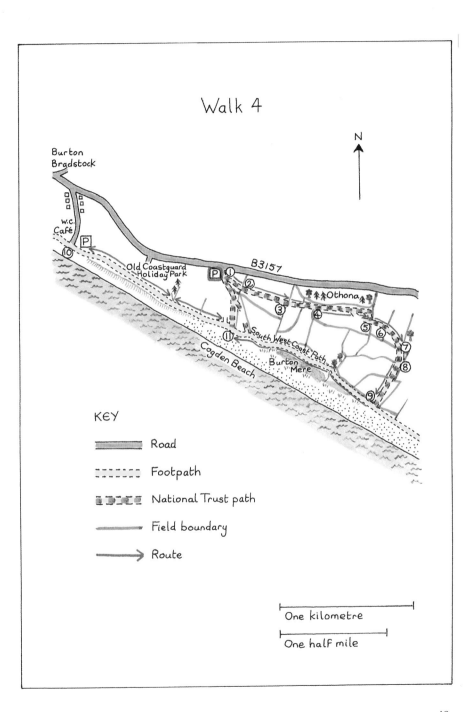

Walk 4

N

Burton
Bradstock

w.c.
Café

P

Old Coastguard
Holiday Park

B3157

Othona

South West Coast Path

Cogden Beach

Burton
Mere

KEY

▰▰▰ Road

┄┄┄ Footpath

▰▰▰ National Trust path

▰▰▰ Field boundary

➤ Route

One kilometre

One half mile

ROUTE

1. Leave the car park by the stile (waymarked "The National Trust") at the top of the lower section - on your left (east) as you face the sea. Cross the stile into a field and follow a footpath heading half right (roughly south-east) down the field for 200 yards (180 metres) until you reach a gate and stile on the far side.

2. Cross the stile into another field and follow the footpath straight ahead of you (roughly east) for 400 yards (360 metres) until you reach a gate and waymarked stile on the far side.
   Bee Orchids and Grass Vetchling can be found in this field.

3. Cross the stile and continue on the footpath (roughly east) across the next two fields for 250 yards (230 metres) until you reach a gate and waymarked stile on the far side of the second field.
   A blue form of Scarlet Pimpernel can sometimes be found in the second field.

4. Cross the stile into the next field and follow the footpath (roughly east) along the left (north) edge for 450 yards (410 metres) until you reach the corner of the field. Turn right (roughly south) and follow the left (east) edge of the field downhill for 50 yards (45 metres) until you reach a gate and waymarked stile on your left.
   Bee and Pyramidal Orchids, Dyer's Greenweed and Grass Vetchling are found in this field.

5. Cross the stile into the next field and follow the footpath which bears right (roughly south-east) for 200 yards (180 metres) until you reach a gate and waymarked stile on the far side.

6. Cross the stile into the next field and follow the path (roughly east then roughly south-east) for 200 yards (180 metres) until you reach a gate and waymarked stile in the far right hand corner.
   This field has many different wild flowers including Dyer's Greenweed, Eyebright, Fairy Flax, Salad Burnet and Wild Thyme.

Left: Scarlet Pimpernel (blue form)

Top: *Grass Vetchling*
Bottom: *Dyer's Greenweed*

7. Cross the stile into the next field; follow the footpath diagonally across (roughly south) for 150 yards (135 metres) downhill to the far left hand corner, where there is a gap in the hedge with a National Trust waymark beside it.

8. Go through the gap and continue downhill (roughly south-west) along the left edge of the next two fields for 400 yards (360 metres) until you reach a gate and waymarked stile at the bottom of the second field.

9. Cross the stile and turn right (roughly north-west) on to a footpath. (This is the coast path, although not waymarked as such here.)

As you cross the stile you will see a large colony of Yellow Irises ahead of you; a few yards to their left (east) you may also find attractive groups of Southern Marsh-orchids.

Follow the coast path (generally north-west) for 1½ miles (2½ km), with good views ahead of you to Golden Cap and the Devon coast, until you reach a car park and café at Burton Bradstock.

Some way along you will emerge on to the Chesil Bank; here you will find special flowers of the shingle, including Sea Beet, Sea Campion, Sea-kale, Sea Sandwort, Thrift - often in breathtaking drifts - and Yellow Horned-poppy.

After passing a caravan site the path takes you along the top of low cliffs with a rich mixture of flowers including Hoary Plantain, Horseshoe Vetch, Kidney Vetch and Pale Flax.

Opposite: *Yellow Iris*

Right: *Southern Marsh-orchid*

The Chesil Bank

"...she drove me to Chesil Beach, where I paddled in a silk sea, and we lay in the sun, in a world where there was nothing, she said, that would have seemed strange to a Roman soldier, or to Dante, or to Milton..."

From *The Diaries of Sylvia Townsend Warner*

The remarkable natural phenomenon of the Chesil Bank (or Beach) runs for over 17 miles (28 km) from Portland in the east to West Bay in the west. It is thought to have been formed at the end of the last Ice Age about 10,000 years ago by rising sea levels bringing debris from landslides to the shore. The pebbles decrease in size from east to west, possibly due to larger pebbles being moved more rapidly than smaller ones by wind-driven waves.

"...the very end of the Chesil Beach, that marks where the huge pebbles that are found at Portland, wide and flat as mill stones, have grown so fine as scarce to serve the turn of two fairies at pains to grind bride-cake-flour out of the seeds of vernal grasses."

From *Dorset Essays*, Llewelyn Powys

The landward side of the bank supports a spectacular variety of wild flowers including Sea Bindweed, Sea Campion, Sea-holly, Sea-kale, Sea Sandwort, Thrift and Yellow Horned-poppy. Many of these plants have fleshy leaves to help them overcome the drying effects of the wind and salt spray at the coast.

Sea-kale

Often found in large colonies on the Chesil Bank, Sea-kale is of special interest as it is one of our few native plants to have been used as a vegetable. The young shoots were blanched by covering and then boiled and served with melted butter.

It became a fashionable delicacy in the late 18th Century and in 1800 Captain Thomas Hardy (later of *The Victory*) obtained supplies from Dorset for Lady Nelson.

In Dorset Sea-kale is found mostly in the west of the county on shingle or sandy beaches and, sometimes, on cliffs. Fully grown plants are around 2 feet (60 cm) tall and 4 feet (120 cm) across. The sweet-smelling white flowers have 4 petals, measure about ½ inch (1¼ cm) across and are borne in large clusters. The leaves are pale bluish green, fleshy and wavy-edged.

10.   Retrace your steps back along the coast path (roughly south-east) for ¾ mile (1¼ km), with spectacular views along the Chesil Bank to Portland, until you reach a track going off to your left.

11.   Turn left (roughly north) on to the track and follow it uphill for 450 yards (410 metres) until you reach the car park.

Above: Sea-kale
Opposite: Looking west along the Chesil Bank towards Golden Cap - Thrift, Common Bird's-foot-trefoil and Sea-kale

Yellow Horned-poppy

"A poppy grows upon the shore,
Bursts her twin cup in summer late:
Her leaves are glaucous-green and hoar,
Her petals yellow, delicate.

Oft to her cousins turns her thought,
In wonder if they care that she
Is fed with spray for dew, and caught
By every gale that sweeps the sea.

She has no lovers like the red,
That dances with the noble corn:
Her blossoms on the waves are shed,
Where she stands shivering and forlorn."

Robert Bridges (Poet Laureate 1913-30)

Robert Bridges aptly captures the hostile conditions of the shingle beach where this attractive and remarkable flower grows. Found all along the Dorset coast on sand, clay undercliffs and chalk cliff tops, as well as shingle, its bright yellow flowers stand out at a considerable distance. Up to 2½ inches (6cm) across, they have 4 delicate, silky petals surrounding a prominent mass of yellow stamens.

The leaves are a pale bluish green, slightly fleshy and very hairy. Their wavy edges and irregular shapes, together with the long curved "horns" of the seed pods, add to the strange appeal of this plant.

Some of the flowers you may see on this walk

Bee Orchid *(Ophrys apifera)*
Bittersweet, Woody Nightshade
 (Solanum dulcamara)
Black Medick *(Medicago lupulina)*
Buck's-horn Plantain
 (Plantago coronopus)
Bugle *(Ajuga reptans)*
Bulbous Buttercup
 (Ranunculus bulbosus)
Cat's-ear *(Hypochaeris radicata)*
Changing Forget-me-not
 (Myosotis discolor)
Cleavers, Sticky Willy
 (Galium aparine)
Common Bird's-foot-trefoil, Eggs-and-
 Bacon *(Lotus corniculatus)*
Common Dog-violet *(Viola riviniana)*
Common Centaury
 (Centaurium erythraea)
Common Field-speedwell
 (Veronica persica)
Common Mallow *(Malva sylvestris)*
Common Milkwort *(Polygala vulgaris)*
Common Mouse-ear
 (Cerastium fontanum)
Common Sorrel *(Rumex acetosa)*
Common Vetch *(Vicia sativa)*
Cowslip *(Primula veris)*
Creeping Buttercup
 (Ranunculus repens)
Creeping Cinquefoil
 (Potentilla reptans)
Cuckooflower *(Cardamine pratensis)*
Cut-leaved Crane's-bill
 (Geranium dissectum)

Daisy *(Bellis perennis)*
Dandelions *(Taraxacum agg.)*
Dove's-foot Crane's-bill
 (Geranium molle)
Dyer's Greenweed *(Genista tinctoria)*
Eyebright *(Euphrasia officinalis agg.)*
Fairy Flax *(Linum catharticum)*
Field Bindweed *(Convolvulus arvensis)*
Field Forget-me-not
 (Myosotis arvensis)
Germander Speedwell
 (Veronica chamaedrys)
Gorse *(Ulex europaeus)*
Grass Vetchling *(Lathyrus nissolia)*
Ground-ivy *(Glechoma hederacea)*
Hedge Bindweed *(Calystegia sepium)*
Hedge Woundwort *(Stachys sylvatica)*
Hemlock Water-dropwort
 (Oenanthe crocata)
Herb-Robert *(Geranium robertianum)*
Hoary Cress *(Lepidum draba)*
Hoary Plantain *(Plantago media)*
Hogweed *(Heracleum sphondylium)*
Horseshoe Vetch *(Hippocrepis comosa)*
Kidney Vetch *(Anthyllis vulneraria)*
Lesser Trefoil *(Trifolium dubium)*
Meadow Buttercup *(Ranunculus acris)*
Mouse-ear-hawkweed
 (Pilosella officinarum)
Pale Flax *(Linum bienne)*
Parsley-piert *(Aphanes arvensis)*
Prickly Sow-thistle *(Sonchus asper)*
Pyramidal Orchid
 (Anacamptis pyramidalis)
Red Clover *(Trifolium pratense)*

Previous pages
Left: *Yellow Horned-poppy on the Chesil Bank*
Right: *Sea Campion*

58

Red Dead-nettle *(Lamium purpureum)*
Ribwort Plantain *(Plantago lanceolata)*
Rough Clover *(Trifolium scabrum)*
Salad Burnet *(Sanguisorba minor*
    ssp. *minor)*
Scarlet Pimpernel *(Anagallis arvensis*
    ssp. *arvensis)*
Sea Beet *(Beta vulgaris* ssp. *maritima)*
Sea Campion *(Silene uniflora)*
Sea-kale *(Crambe maritima)*
Sea Sandwort *(Honckenya peploides)*
Selfheal *(Prunella vulgaris)*
Silverweed *(Potentilla anserina)*
Slender Thistle *(Carduus tenuiflorus)*
Small-flowered Buttercup
    (Ranunculus parviflorus)
Spotted Medick *(Medicago arabica)*
Southern Marsh-orchid
    (Dactylorhiza praetermissa)

Stinking Iris, Gladdon
    (Iris foetidissima)
Thrift, Sea Pink *(Armeria maritima)*
Thyme-leaved Speedwell
    (Veronica serpyllifolia)
Tufted Vetch *(Vicia cracca)*
Wall Speedwell *(Veronica arvensis)*
White Campion *(Silene latifolia)*
White Clover *(Trifolium repens)*
Wild Carrot *(Daucus carota* ssp.
    carota)
Wild Parsnip *(Pastinaca sativa* var.
    sativa)
Wild Rose *(Rosa agg.)*
Wild Thyme *(Thymus polytrichus)*
Yellow Horned-poppy
    (Glaucium flavum)
Yellow Iris *(Iris pseudacorus)*

Right: *Hoary Plantain*

59

WALK 5

SUMMER ORCHIDS ON AN IRON AGE HILL-FORT
Eggardon Hill and Spyway

An early summer walk on and around a chalk downland hill-fort in West Dorset. Starting close to Eggardon Hill, we walk round its well-preserved banks and ditches. From the hill we have outstanding views to the south-west along the West Dorset and Devon coasts and to the west and north-west towards Coney's Castle, Lambert's Castle, Pilsdon Pen and Lewesdon Hill.

We then descend over downland and along a track to the hamlet of Spyway, before climbing again to approach Eggardon Hill from the west. Finally, we skirt the northern edge of the hill-fort on a minor road before returning to our starting point.

We see many flowers of the chalk on Eggardon Hill, including four types of orchid. Elsewhere, we find a wide variety of early summer flowers.

Time of year:	June
Distance:	about 6 miles (10 km)
Difficulty:	fairly strenuous with some hills
Parking:	small parking area at the Shatcombe Lane Picnic Area, beside minor road, at SY 549 948 (free)
Directions to car park:	from the roundabout at the eastern side of Bridport take the A35 eastwards. After 2½ miles (4 km) take a left turn (signposted "Askerswell 1½ Maiden Newton 7"). After ½ mile (¾ km) turn right at a junction, passing the Spyway Inn on your right after another ¾ mile (1¼ km). After a further 1½ miles (2½ km) continue straight ahead at a crossroads before turning right 220 yards (200 metres) further on (signposted "Wynford Eagle 2½ Maiden Newton 4¼"): you will find the parking area on your left after about 200 yards (180 metres).
Ordnance Survey maps:	1:50,000 Landranger 194 Dorchester and Weymouth 1:25,000 Explorer OL 15 Purbeck & South Dorset 1:25,000 Explorer 117 Cerne Abbas & Bere Regis
Public transport:	None
Refreshments:	In Spyway
Toilets:	None

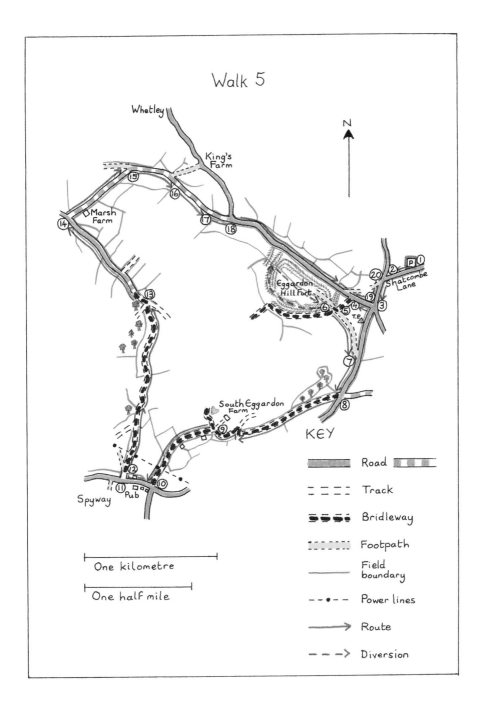

Walk 5

N

Whetley

King's Farm

Marsh Farm

Eggardon Hill Fort

Shatcombe Lane

P

South Eggardon Farm

KEY

Spyway

Pub

T.P.

KEY

Road

Track

Bridleway

Footpath

Field boundary

Power lines

Route

Diversion

One kilometre

One half mile

ROUTE

1. From the parking area turn right (roughly west) along the road and continue until you reach a junction.
2. Turn left (roughly south) at the junction (signposted "Askerswell ½ Bridport 5") and follow the road for 220 yards (200 metres) until you reach a crossroads.
   Field Scabious is found on the left hand verge here.
3. Turn right (roughly north-west) at the crossroads (signposted "Powerstock West Milton") and follow the road for 220 yards (200 metres) until you reach a gate and bridleway sign on your left.
4. Go through the gate into a field and follow the bridleway (roughly south-west) across the field for 150 yards (135 metres) until you reach a gate on the other side.
5. Go through the gate. Turn right (roughly west) and continue on the bridleway for a few yards until you reach a gate and waymarked stile at the entrance to Eggardon Hill. (There is a National Trust information board here.)

Below: *View south-west and west from the banks of Eggardon hill-fort towards Thorncombe Beacon and Golden Cap.*

Eggardon Hill

"But there on the hill-crest,
Where only larks or stars look down,
Earthworks exposed a vaster nest,
Its race of men long flown."

From *A Prehistoric Camp*,
Andrew Young

Although perhaps not as spectacular a hill-fort as Hambledon Hill (see Walk 3), Eggardon Hill makes up for this with its exceptional views.

Start at the stile (stage 5 of the route) and walk clockwise around the hill-fort along one of the banks. You will soon have fine views south to Abbotsbury Castle (another Iron Age hill-fort) and Pins Knoll, topped by a small building.

To the south-west and west are excellent views towards the sea, with Shipton Hill, Thorncombe Beacon, Golden Cap and the Devon coast visible on a clear day.

As you continue along the south side of the hill-fort, notice the great depth of the ditches compared with their enclosing banks:

"...ramparts so lofty that you can eat your lunch (as I have done)
in the outer ditch with no more than a zephyr straying to your
cheeks from the gale overhead."

From *The English Downland*,
H.J. Massingham

As you move round to the south-west side of the hill-fort, the view to the west and north-west opens up. Over the patchwork of small fields typical of West Dorset you see Colmer's and Hardown Hills, Coney's Castle (see Walk 1) and Lambert's Castle, while a little further north are Pilsdon Pen and Lewesdon Hill. The north-east part of the hill-fort is in private ownership and the return route to your starting point is along the boundary fence between the two parts.

Wild flowers are abundant on the banks - as with other hill-forts the absence of ploughing and other agricultural operations have allowed a great diversity of flowers to flourish. Four species of orchid - Bee, Common Spotted-, Fragrant and Pyramidal - can be found along the banks on the south side. Other attractive flowers seen on the hill-fort include Dwarf Thistle, Eyebright, Fairy Flax, Horseshoe Vetch, Salad Burnet, Squinancywort and Wild Thyme.

Bee Orchid

"I saw a bee, I saw a flower;
I looked again and said, For sure
Never was flower, never was bee
Locked in such immobility.

The loud bees lurched about the hill,
But this flower-buried bee was still;
I said, O Love, has love the power
To change a bee into a flower."

The Bee-Orchis,
Andrew Young

With its velvety brown and yellow lip the Bee Orchid does look remarkably like a bumble-bee resting on a pink flower. In Mediterranean countries bees pollinate the flowers of similar species by attempting to mate with them, although in this country Bee Orchids are self-pollinating.

The flowers measure about 1 inch (2½ cm) across and there are usually five or more to each spike. The leaves are light green, narrow and pointed, the upper clasping the stem and the lower in a rosette at the base.

Found in Dorset in chalk and limestone turf, Bee Orchid numbers vary considerably from year to year.

6.   Leave the hill-fort area by the stile where you entered. Continue straight ahead on a grassy track and follow this (roughly south-east and then south) for 450 yards (410 metres) until you reach a road.

7.   Turn right (roughly south) on to the road and follow it downhill (roughly south-west) for 350 yards (320 metres) until you reach a gate and bridleway on your right.

8.   Turn right (roughly west) through the gate on to the bridleway and follow it (roughly west) for just over ½ mile (1 km) until you reach a gate leading on to a made-up track.

Opposite: *Bee Orchid*

9.   Go through the gate, turn left (west) on to the track and follow it (roughly west and then roughly south-west) for 800 yards (730 metres) until you reach a road.

10.   Turn right (roughly north-west) at the road and follow it downhill (roughly west) for 220 yards (200 metres), passing the Spyway Inn on your left, until you reach a track on your right.

11.   Turn right (roughly north-east) on to the track and follow it for 25 yards (23 metres) until you reach a gate ahead of you and a sign for a bridleway.

12.   Go through the gate into a field, ignoring a footpath going to the left. Follow the bridleway (generally north) for about ¾ mile (1¼ km), going through a further three fields, until you reach a partly made-up track crossing ahead of you.

13.   Turn left (roughly north-west) on to the track, signposted "Bridleway Powerstock ½" and follow it (roughly north-west) for just over ½ mile (nearly 1 km) - the track soon becomes a made-up road - until you reach a junction with a track on your right. As you walk downhill you have a good view of Lewesdon Hill ahead of you.
      Hedgerow Crane's-bill grows in the verge to your right shortly before the junction.

Opposite: *Musk Thistle, Nodding Thistle*
Below: *Wild Rose*

14. Turn right (roughly north-east) on to the track (signposted "Marsh Farm Eggardon Hill ¾") and follow it uphill, passing Marsh Farm on your right, for 600 yards (550 metres) until you reach a junction with a footpath on your left.

    Wood Spurge can be found in the hedgerow on your right after about 400 yards (360 metres).

15. Continue on the track (signposted "Bridleway Eggardon Hill ½") as it bears right (roughly east). Follow it uphill (roughly east then roughly south-east), going through a gate after 200 yards (180 metres), until, after a further 200 yards (180 metres), you reach a second gate.

16. Go through the gate and continue on the track (roughly south-east), with the western edge of Eggardon Hill ahead of you, for a further 450 yards (410 metres) until you reach another gate.

17. Go through the gate and continue on the track (roughly east) for 150 yards (135 metres) until you reach a road.

18. Continue straight ahead on to the road and follow it uphill (roughly east then roughly south-east) for nearly a mile (1½ km), skirting the northern edge of Eggardon Hill, until you reach a crossroads.

    Fine groups of Common Spotted-orchids can be found on the verges of this road.

19. Turn left (roughly north) at the crossroads (signposted "Toller Porcorum Maiden Newton") and follow the road for 220 yards (200 metres) until you reach a road junction on your right.

20. Turn right (roughly east) at the junction (signposted "Wynford Eagle 2½ Maiden Newton 4¼") and continue along the road until you reach the parking area on your left.

Opposite: *Goat's-beard*

> *With its very narrow leaves and flowers only fully open on sunny mornings, the presence of this intriguing plant is often only betrayed by its large dandelion-like seed clocks.*

Some of the flowers you may see on this walk

Agrimony *(Agrimonia eupatoria)*
Bee Orchid *(Ophrys apifera)*
Bittersweet, Woody Nightshade
    (Solanum dulcamara)
Black Medick *(Medicago lupulina)*
Broad-leaved Dock
    (Rumex obtusifolius)
Broad-leaved Willowherb
    (Epilobium montanum)
Bulbous Buttercup
    (Ranunculus bulbosus)
Burnet-saxifrage *(Pimpinella saxifraga)*
Bush Vetch *(Vicia sepium)*
Cat's-ear *(Hypochaeris radicata)*
Cleavers, Sticky Willy
    (Galium aparine)
Common Bird's-foot-trefoil, Eggs-and-
    Bacon *(Lotus corniculatus)*
Common Field-speedwell
    (Veronica persica)
Common Knapweed, Hardheads
    (Centaurea nigra)
Common Mallow *(Malva sylvestris)*
Common Milkwort *(Polygala vulgaris)*
Common Mouse-ear
    (Cerastium fontanum)
Common Poppy *(Papaver rhoeas)*
Common Restharrow *(Ononis repens)*
Common Sorrel *(Rumex acetosa)*
Common Spotted-orchid
    (Dactylorhiza fuchsii)
Creeping Buttercup
    (Ranunculus repens)
Creeping Cinquefoil
    (Potentilla reptans)
Creeping Thistle *(Cirsium arvense)*
Crosswort *(Cruciata laevipes)*
Cut-leaved Crane's-bill
    (Geranium dissectum)

Daisy *(Bellis perennis)*
Dandelions *(Taraxacum agg.)*
Dove's-foot Crane's-bill
    (Geranium molle)
Dwarf Thistle, Stemless Thistle
    (Cirsium acaule)
Eyebright *(Euphrasia officinalis agg.)*
Fairy Flax *(Linum catharticum)*
Field Bindweed *(Convolvulus arvensis)*
Field Forget-me-not
    (Myosotis arvensis)
Field Scabious *(Knautia arvensis)*
Fragrant Orchid
    (Gymnadenia conopsea)
Foxglove *(Digitalis purpurea)*
Germander Speedwell
    (Veronica chamaedrys)
Goat's-beard *(Tragopogon pratensis*
    ssp. *minor)*
Ground-ivy *(Glechoma hederacea)*
Heath Bedstraw *(Galium saxatile)*
Hedge Bedstraw *(Galium mollugo)*
Hedge Woundwort *(Stachys sylvatica)*
Hedgerow Crane's-bill
    (Geranium pyrenaicum)
Herb-Robert *(Geranium robertianum)*
Hoary Plantain *(Plantago media)*
Hogweed *(Heracleum sphondylium)*
Horseshoe Vetch *(Hippocrepis comosa)*
Lady's Bedstraw *(Galium verum)*
Lesser Stitchwort *(Stellaria graminea)*
Marsh Thistle *(Cirsium palustre)*
Meadow Buttercup *(Ranunculus acris)*
Meadow Vetchling *(Lathyrus pratensis)*
Mouse-ear-hawkweed
    (Pilosella officinarum)
Musk Thistle, Nodding Thistle
    (Carduus nutans)

Oxeye Daisy *(Leucanthemum vulgare)*
Perforate St. John's-wort
    (Hypericum perforatum)
Pineappleweed *(Matricaria discoidea)*
Prickly Sow-thistle *(Sonchus asper)*
Pyramidal Orchid
    (Anacamptis pyramidalis)
Red Campion *(Silene dioica)*
Red Clover *(Trifolium pratense)*
Ribwort Plantain *(Plantago lanceolata)*
Sainfoin *(Onobrychis viciifolia)*
Salad Burnet *(Sanguisorba minor*
    ssp. *minor)*
Scarlet Pimpernel *(Anagallis arvensis*
    ssp. *arvensis)*
Selfheal *(Prunella vulgaris)*
Shepherd's-purse *(Capsella*
    bursa-pastoris)
Silverweed *(Potentilla anserina)*
Small Scabious *(Scabiosa columbaria)*
Squinancywort *(Asperula cynanchica)*
Stinking Iris, Gladdon
    (Iris foetidissima)
Tufted Vetch *(Vicia cracca)*
White Clover *(Trifolium repens)*
Wild Marjoram *(Origanum vulgare)*
Wild Rose *(Rosa agg.)*
Wild Thyme *(Thymus polytrichus)*
Wood Avens, Herb Bennet
    (Geum urbanum)
Wood Spurge
    (Euphorbia amygdaloides)
Yarrow *(Achillea millefolium)*
Yellow Iris *(Iris pseudacorus)*

Top right: *Common Spotted-orchid*
Bottom right: *Pyramidal Orchid*

WALK 6

WATER-LILIES ALONG A SLOW DORSET RIVER
The River Stour at Sturminster Newton

A midsummer walk along and around a slow-moving river in North Dorset. Starting in the centre of Sturminster Newton, we make our way through this attractive town and down to the River Stour. We then follow the river north for 1½ miles (2½ km) until we reach the ruins of Cutt Mill.

We cross the river and walk across fields towards Pentridge Farm where, as a boy, the poet William Barnes often visited his aunt and uncle. We then follow lanes and minor roads for 2½ miles (4 km) before reaching the river again at Sturminster Mill.

We cross again and head back to the town along a footpath close to the river, passing Thomas Hardy's house on our way. Finally, we retrace our steps up to the town centre and the car park.

We see a variety of interesting water plants along the river including Fringed, White and Yellow Water-lilies, Arrowhead, Branched Bur-reed, Flowering-rush and Purple-loosestrife.

Time of year:	July
Distance:	about 6 miles (10 km)
Difficulty:	fairly easy with few hills; can be muddy in places
Parking:	car park in centre of Sturminster Newton at ST 788 142 (free)
Directions to car park:	from the A357 take the B3092 to Sturminster Newton town centre. After ½ mile (¾ km) turn right into Station Road (B3091). After 75 yards (70 metres) turn right and the car park is on your left.
Ordnance Survey maps:	1:50,000 Landranger 183 Yeovil & Frome 1:50,000 Landranger 194 Dorchester & Weymouth 1:25,000 Explorer 129 Yeovil & Sherborne
Public transport:	buses to Sturminster Newton from many parts of Dorset (check timetable)
Refreshments:	in Sturminster Newton
Toilets:	at car park and Sturminster Mill

Walk 6

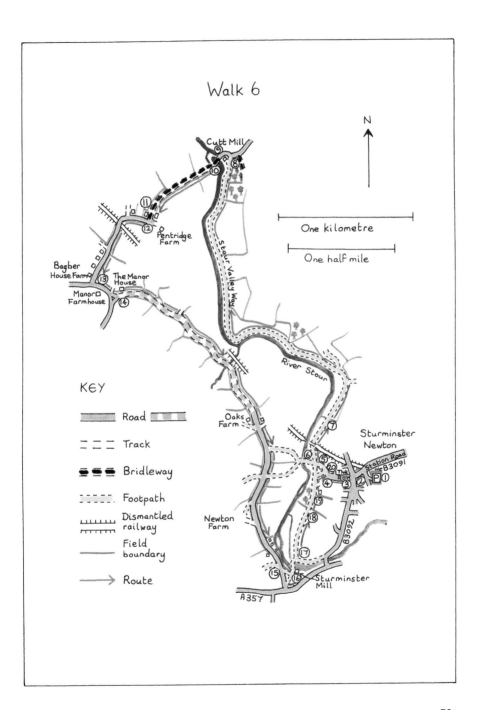

N

Cutt Mill

Stour Valley Way

One kilometre

One half mile

Pentridge Farm

Bagber House Farm

The Manor House

Manor Farmhouse

River Stour

KEY

Road

Track

Bridleway

Footpath

Dismantled railway

Field boundary

Route

Oaks Farm

Sturminster Newton

Station Road inc B3091

The Row

Newton Farm

B3092

Sturminster Mill

A357

The River Stour

"I followed each detour
Of the slow meadow-winding Stour,
That looked on cloud, tree, hill,
And mostly flowed by standing still."

From *The Slow Race*,
Andrew Young

As you walk along the bank of the River Stour here in summer the movement of water is often hardly visible. It is this gentle flow which contributes to the abundance of flowers found in it and along its edges. Plants have difficulty in rooting in fast-flowing water but in slow-moving rivers such as the Stour many species are able to grow.

Flowers found in the open water include Amphibious Bistort, Arrowhead and Fringed, White and Yellow Water-lilies, while along the edges are Branched Bur-reed, Flowering-rush, Marsh Woundwort and Purple-loosestrife.

ROUTE

1. Turn right (roughly north-west) on leaving the car park and follow the road until you reach a junction.
2. Turn left (roughly west) into Station Road and continue for 75 yards (70 metres) until you reach Market Place.
3. Cross over the road into the narrow road opposite (The Row), which runs just to the right of Barclays Bank. The road is waymarked "The Stour Valley Way", which you will be following until stage 8. Follow this road (roughly west) for 250 yards (230 metres) until you reach a kissing gate at the far end.
4. Go through the kissing gate and follow a footpath (signposted "Colber Bridge ¼ Road Lane Farm 1½") downhill (roughly north-west) for 100 yards (90 metres) until you reach another kissing gate.
5. Go through the kissing gate and after a few yards turn right (roughly north) on to a crossing footpath (signposted "Hinton St. Mary 1½").
6. Follow the footpath (roughly north then roughly north-east) for 450 yards (410 metres), passing under the waymarked right hand arch of a former railway bridge and continue until you reach a waymarked stile. *You will see a large group of Yellow Irises to your left just before reaching the stile.*
7. Cross the stile and continue to follow the waymarked footpath (generally north, then west and finally north again) for about 1½ miles (2½ km) close to or along the bank of the River Stour, until, at the end of a wooded section, you reach a stile with a lane beyond. You will have good views of the river as you go along. *You will find many water plants along the river including Arrowhead, Branched Bur-reed, Flowering-rush, Fringed Water-lily, Marsh Woundwort and Yellow Water-lily.*
8. Cross the stile (waymarked to show the Stour Valley Way straight ahead) and, leaving the Stour Valley Way, turn left (roughly north-west) down the lane. Continue down the lane for 100 yards (90 metres) until, just past a thatched cottage on your left, you reach the ruins of Cutt Mill.

Opposite: The River Stour near Sturminster Newton

9. With the ruins on your right, cross the bridge over the river and continue for a few yards until you reach a gate (waymarked for a bridleway).
Arrowhead, Purple-loosestrife, White Water-lily and Yellow Water-lily are found here. There are also several pairs of kingfishers in the area.

10. Go through the gate and follow the bridleway (roughly south-west) for 650 yards (590 metres) over two fields and between two fences beside a third field until you reach a gate at some farm buildings close to a house. Just before reaching the gate you will see Pentridge Farm on your left.

11. Go through the gate, past the farm buildings, through another gate and turn right (roughly west) into a lane.

12. Follow the lane (roughly west then roughly south-west) for about ½ mile (¾ km), crossing over the path of the old railway after 300 yards (270 metres), until you reach a junction with a road.

13. Turn left (roughly east) on to the road and follow it for 100 yards (90 metres) until it bears right at a triangle of roads at a junction with a track.

Top right: *Marsh Woundwort*

Middle right: *Arrowhead*

Bottom right: *Branched Bur-reed*

Opposite: *The River Stour near Cutt Mill*

14. Turn left (east) along the track (signposted "Halter path to Sturminster Newton"). Follow the track, which eventually becomes a made-up road, (east then generally south-east) for about 2 miles (about 3 km) until, shortly before it reaches the A357 road, you reach a footpath on the left signposted "Sturminster Mill".
Elecampane can be found on the left part way along the track.

15. Turn left (roughly south-east) on to the footpath, go through a kissing gate and follow the footpath for 75 yards (70 metres) through a picnic area, taking the left hand (lower) branch which emerges at the mill building.

16. Turn left (north), go past the mill building on your right and across three bridges over the River Stour until you reach a kissing gate.
Arrowhead, Marsh Woundwort and Yellow Water-lily are found in the river here.

17. Go through the kissing gate into a field and take the footpath straight ahead (roughly north), signposted "Colber Bridge ½", ignoring the footpath to the right (signposted "Town Bridge ¼"). Follow the footpath (roughly north) for 450 yards (410 metres) across the field until you reach a kissing gate on the far side.

Opposite: *Flowering-rush*
Below: *Sturminster Mill*

Yellow Water-lily

"O zummer clote! when the brook's a-glidèn
So slow an' smooth down his zedgy bed,
Upon thy broad leaves so seäfe a-ridèn
The water's top wi' thy yollow head,"

From *The Clote*,
William Barnes

William Barnes was brought up at Bagber, about two miles west of Sturminster Newton, and went to school in the town. He would have crossed the Stour on his way and seen large areas of the slow-moving river covered by Yellow Water-lilies - his "clotes".

The cup-shaped flowers are bright yellow, up to about 3 inches (7½ cm) across and held on long stalks protruding from the water; the fruits are green and shaped like wine carafes. The visible leaves are pale green, very large, nearly heart-shaped and float on the surface of the water.

In Dorset, the Yellow Water-lily is widespread in slow-moving rivers and streams.

18.   Go through the kissing gate and follow the footpath (roughly north-east) across a recreation ground for 100 yards (90 metres) until you reach a kissing gate on the far side.
19.   Go through the kissing gate and follow the footpath (roughly north), signposted "Colber Bridge ½ Hinton St. Mary 1½", passing Thomas Hardy's house (believed to be the left of the pair) on your right. After 200 yards (180 metres), the footpath forks for a second time (ignore the first fork after 75 yards (70 metres)). Follow the right hand fork until you reach a stile after a few yards.
20.   Cross the stile and turn right (roughly south-east) on to a footpath (signposted "Market Place ¼"). Follow the path uphill (roughly south-east) for 100 yards (90 metres) until you reach a kissing gate. Go through the kissing gate on to the road and retrace your steps to the car park along The Row, over Market Place and along Station Road. Hambledon Hill (see Walk 3) can be seen roughly to the east from the car park.

Opposite: Yellow Water-lily

Some of the flowers you may see on this walk

Agrimony *(Agrimonia eupatoria)*
Amphibious Bistort
   (Persicaria amphibia)
Arrowhead *(Sagittaria sagittifolia)*
Black Medick *(Medicago lupulina)*
Branched Bur-reed
   (Sparganium erectum)
Cleavers, Sticky Willy
   (Galium aparine)
Comfreys *(Symphytum agg.)*
Common Centaury
   (Centaurium erythraea)
Common Knapweed, Hardheads
   (Centaurea nigra)
Common Mallow *(Malva sylvestris)*
Creeping Buttercup
   (Ranunculus repens)
Creeping Cinquefoil
   (Potentilla reptans)
Creeping-Jenny
   (Lysimachia nummularia)
Cut-leaved Crane's-bill
   (Geranium dissectum)
Elecampane *(Inula helenium)*
Field Bindweed *(Convolvulus arvensis)*
Flowering-rush *(Butomus umbellatus)*
Fringed Water-lily
   (Nymphoides peltata)
Great Mullein *(Verbascum thapsus)*
Great Willowherb *(Epilobium hirsutum)*
Gypsywort *(Lycopus europaeus)*
Hairy St. John's-wort
   (Hypericum hirsutum)
Hedge Bedstraw *(Galium mollugo)*
Hedge Bindweed *(Calystegia sepium)*
Hedge Woundwort *(Stachys sylvatica)*
Hemlock *(Conium maculatum)*
Hemlock Water-dropwort
   (Oenanthe crocata)

Herb-Robert *(Geranium robertianum)*
Hogweed *(Heracleum sphondylium)*
Lesser Burdock *(Arctium minus)*
Lesser Stitchwort *(Stellaria graminea)*
Marsh Thistle *(Cirsium palustre)*
Marsh Woundwort *(Stachys palustris)*
Meadow Crane's-bill
   (Geranium pratense)
Meadowsweet *(Filipendula ulmaria)*
Meadow Vetchling *(Lathyrus pratensis)*
Nipplewort *(Lapsana communis)*
Oxeye Daisy *(Leucanthemum vulgare)*
Pink Water-speedwell
   (Veronica catenata)
Purple-loosestrife *(Lythrum salicaria)*
Red Campion *(Silene dioica)*
Red Clover *(Trifolium pratense)*
Redshank *(Persicaria maculosa)*
Ribwort Plantain *(Plantago lanceolata)*
Scentless Mayweed
   (Tripleurospermum inodorum)
Selfheal *(Prunella vulgaris)*
Shining Crane's-bill
   (Geranium lucidum)
Silverweed *(Potentilla anserina)*
Spear Thistle *(Cirsium vulgare)*
Tufted Vetch *(Vicia cracca)*
Water Chickweed
   (Myosoton aquaticum)
Water Figwort
   (Scrophularia auriculata)
Water Forget-me-not
   (Myosotis scorpioides)
Water-plantain *(Alisma plantago-*
   aquatica)
Welted Thistle *(Carduus crispus)*
White Clover *(Trifolium repens)*
White Dead-nettle *(Lamium album)*
White Water-lily *(Nymphaea alba)*

Wild Teasel *(Dipsacus fullonum)*
Wood Avens, Herb Bennet
    (Geum urbanum)

Yarrow *(Achillea millefolium)*
Yellow Iris *(Iris pseudacorus)*
Yellow Water-lily *(Nuphar lutea)*

Below: *Purple-loosestrife*

WALK 7

GOLDEN-SAMPHIRE AND PORTLAND SEA-LAVENDER ON DORSET'S SOUTHERN TIP
Round and about Portland Bill

A late summer walk on the coast path around the southern tip of Portland. Starting 2 miles (3 km) north-east of Portland Bill we join the path after a short walk along a road. We then follow the coast path along the east side of Portland through disused limestone quarries, past Cave Hole and Portland Bill Lighthouse to the very tip of the Bill.

Turning north we pass Portland Raised Beach and follow the coast path along the top of the cliffs on the west side of the island. We pass the disused Old Higher Lighthouse and have good views north-west to the Chesil Bank and the West Dorset coast. Turning inland, we follow a footpath for a short distance before making our way along roads through Southwell and back to the car park.

We see a great variety of flowers on the limestone along the coast path, including Portland Sea-lavender - found only on the island - and large numbers of the nationally scarce Golden-samphire, together with Carline Thistle, Greater, Lesser and Rock Sea-spurreys, Ploughman's-spikenard, Portland Spurge and Rock Samphire.

Time of year:	mid-July to late August
Distance:	about 4 miles (6½ km)
Difficulty:	easy with no appreciable hills
Parking:	Cheyne Weares car park at SY 693 705 (free)
Directions to car park:	take the A354 south through Easton; continue on the road towards Portland Bill, passing Portland Museum on your left. About 300 yards (270 metres) after the museum you will see a turn signposted "Weston ½" on your right. The car park is on your left about 600 yards (550 metres) past this turn.
Ordnance Survey maps:	1:50,000 Landranger 194 Dorchester & Weymouth 1:25,000 Explorer OL 15 Purbeck & South Dorset
Public transport:	X10, 501 buses to Portland Bill from Weymouth (check timetable)
Refreshments:	at Portland Bill and in Southwell
Toilets:	at Portland Bill

Walk 7

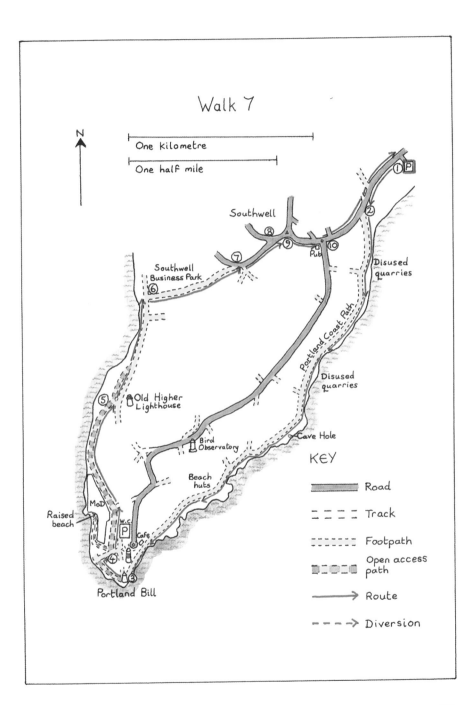

N

One kilometre

One half mile

Southwell

① ②

Disused quarries

Southwell Business Park

⑥ ⑦

⑧ ⑨ ⑩ Pub

Portland Coast Path

Disused quarries

Old Higher Lighthouse

⑤

Bird Observatory

Cave Hole

KEY

Beach huts

Raised beach

MoD

W.C.

P Cafe

④ ③

Portland Bill

▬▬▬	Road
─ ─ ─ ─	Track
-------	Footpath
▭▭▭▭	Open access path
───→	Route
- - - →	Diversion

ROUTE

1. Turn left (roughly south-west) on leaving the car park and follow the road for 400 yards (360 metres) until you see a sign for the coast path on your left.

2. Take the coast path and follow it (generally south-west) for 1½ miles (2½ km) along the east side of the island to the Trinity House seamark (marked "TH 1844") at the tip of the Bill, passing the red and white Portland Bill Lighthouse on your right. The path first takes you through an area of old quarries; about 250 yards (230 metres) past the final quarry you will find Cave Hole on your left.

Many wild flowers are found along the path; especially prominent are Golden-samphire and Portland Sea-lavender. Other flowers you will see include Carline Thistle, Fennel, Ploughman's-spikenard, Portland Spurge, Red Valerian and Rock Samphire.

Cave Hole

"...the treacherous cavern known as Cave Hole, into which the sea roared and splashed now as it had done when they visited it together as children."

From *The Well-Beloved*, Thomas Hardy

Hardy's "treacherous cavern" is found on the seaward side of the coast path along the east of the island (grid reference: SY 686 690). There is no sign of it until you are almost there as the hole is in the centre of a depression in the ground: it leads down to a cave beneath, where the relentless sea has undermined the cliffs.

The hole used to be perilously open and in rough weather the sea would spout through it; it has now been covered with iron bars and stone blocks heaped on top, but there remain some small gaps through which the sea can still be seen.

Large groups of Golden-samphire grow in the depression surrounding the hole.

3. Turn right (roughly north-west) just before the seamark and follow the coast path around the tip of the Bill until, after 200 yards (180 metres), it turns right at a waymarked stone. While walking round the tip of the Bill notice the rough water just out to sea - this is the meeting place of opposing tides, called the "Race":

> "The thick lids of Night closed upon me
> Alone at the Bill
> Of the Isle by the Race -
> Many-caverned, bald, wrinkled of face -"
>
> From *The Souls of the Slain*,
> Thomas Hardy

Above: Portland Bill Lighthouse

Opposite: Cave Hole with Golden-samphire

Portland Sea-lavender

Portland Sea-lavender is one of several Rock Sea-lavenders found in Britain. What makes it special is that it is found only in a small area around Portland Bill. You will see it frequently along the route - particularly on the cliffs and in the disused quarries on the east side of the island.

These charming plants are often quite small - sometimes no more than 4 inches (10 cm) tall - and have branched densely-packed spikes of attractive purplish flowers.

The leaves are small with pointed tips and grow in rosettes at the base of the plant. They have a waxy coating, giving them a bluish green appearance and helping the plant to retain fresh water in the harsh conditions where it grows.

Opposite: Portland Sea-lavender
Below left: Common Knapweed (form with "rays")
Below right: Red Valerian beside the coast path

4. Continue to follow the coast path to the right of a high wire fence (roughly north-east then roughly north-west).

    To visit the Portland Raised Beach turn left (west) just before the fence and walk along its south side; turn right (north) at the corner and walk carefully along the top of the cliff. The raised beach is to your right inside the fence; an information board can be found just inside the fence after about 100 yards (90 metres). To rejoin the route retrace your steps to where you left the coast path.

    Continue along the top of the cliffs on the west side of the island (roughly north), reaching the Old Higher Lighthouse on your right after just over ½ mile (1 km).

    Along this section of the path you will see Dwarf Thistle, Squinancywort and dense patches of Wild Carrot. Golden-samphire grows in profusion within the fenced area.

5. Continue (roughly north) on the coast path for a further 550 yards (500 metres) until you reach a footpath on your right (waymarked on a stone) running to the right of a high wire fence. (Ignore the footpath to East Cliff on your right 75 yards (70 metres) before this.) There are fine views here north-west to the Chesil Bank and the West Dorset coast, including Golden Cap.

Below: *Wild Carrot*

Above: *Lesser Burdock*
Below: *Yellow-wort*

Golden-samphire

Golden-samphire grows in such profusion around Portland Bill that, in places, its flattened clusters of deep yellow flowers above dense, bushy foliage dominate the landscape.

Often found on bare limestone rocks close to the sea, exposed to high winds and salt spray, it survives - and thrives - by storing fresh water in its fleshy leaves.

Although frequent in Dorset on chalk and limestone cliffs it is scarce in Britain as a whole.

The daisy-like flowers are about 1 inch (2½ cm) across with golden yellow centres and yellow petals. The leaves are very narrow and often have a three-pointed tip. They pack themselves closely around stiff, upright stems and have a strong, distinctive smell when crushed.

6. Turn right (roughly east) on to the footpath, leaving the coast path. Follow the footpath along the fence (roughly east then roughly north-east) for 550 yards (500 metres) until you reach a road.
    Hoary Plantain can be found just before you reach the road.

7. Turn right (roughly east) on to the road and follow it (roughly east then roughly north-east) downhill for 300 yards (270 metres) until you reach a junction.

8. Turn right (roughly east) at the junction into Sweethill Lane and continue for 75 yards (70 metres) until you reach a triangular junction.

9. Bear right (roughly south-east) at the triangular junction and follow the road (roughly south-east then roughly east) for 200 yards (180 metres) until you reach a mini-roundabout at the Eight Kings public house.

10. Bear left (roughly east) at the mini-roundabout and follow the road, signposted "Easton 1½", (generally north-east) for 700 yards (640 metres) until you reach the car park on your right.

Opposite: Golden-samphire

Some of the flowers you may see on this walk

Agrimony *(Agrimonia eupatoria)*
Bittersweet, Woody Nightshade
   (Solanum dulcamara)
Black Medick *(Medicago lupulina)*
Bristly Oxtongue *(Picris echioides)*
Buck's-horn Plantain
   (Plantago coronopus)
Carline Thistle *(Carlina vulgaris)*
Common Bird's-foot-trefoil, Eggs-and-
   Bacon *(Lotus corniculatus)*
Common Centaury
   (Centaurium erythraea)
Common Fleabane
   (Pulicaria dysenterica)
Common Knapweed, Hardheads
   (Centaurea nigra)
Common Mallow *(Malva sylvestris)*
Common Ragwort *(Senecio jacobaea)*
Common Restharrow *(Ononis repens)*
Common Toadflax *(Linaria vulgaris)*
Creeping Cinquefoil
   (Potentilla reptans)
Creeping Thistle *(Cirsium arvense)*
Dodder *(Cuscuta epithymum)*
Dwarf Thistle, Stemless Thistle
   (Cirsium acaule)
Eyebright *(Euphrasia officinalis agg.)*

Fennel *(Foeniculum vulgare)*
Field Bindweed *(Convolvulus arvensis)*
Field Scabious *(Knautia arvensis)*
Golden-samphire *(Inula crithmoides)*
Greater Knapweed
   (Centaurea scabiosa)
Greater Sea-spurrey
   (Spergularia media)
Hedge Bedstraw *(Galium mollugo)*
Hemp-agrimony
   (Eupatorium cannabinum)
Herb-Robert *(Geranium robertianum)*
Hoary Plantain *(Plantago media)*
Hop Trefoil *(Trifolium campestre)*
Ivy-leaved Toadflax
   (Cymbalaria muralis)
Kidney Vetch *(Anthyllis vulneraria)*
Lady's Bedstraw *(Galium verum)*
Lesser Burdock *(Arctium minus)*
Lesser Centaury
   (Centaurium pulchellum)
Lesser Sea-spurrey
   (Spergularia marina)
Meadow Vetchling *(Lathyrus pratensis)*
Mugwort *(Artemisia vulgaris)*
Pale Flax *(Linum bienne)*
Pellitory-of-the-wall
   (Parietaria judaica)
Perennial Sow-thistle
   (Sonchus arvensis)
Pineappleweed *(Matricaria discoidea)*
Ploughman's-spikenard *(Inula conyzae)*
Portland Sea-lavender *(Limonium
   recurvum* ssp. *recurvum)*
Portland Spurge
   (Euphorbia portlandica)
Prickly Sow-thistle *(Sonchus asper)*
Red Bartsia *(Odontites vernus)*

Red Clover *(Trifolium pratense)*
Red Valerian *(Centranthus ruber)*
Ribwort Plantain *(Plantago lanceolata)*
Rock Samphire *(Crithmum maritimum)*
Rock Sea-spurrey
    (Spergularia rupicola)
Rough Clover *(Trifolium scabrum)*
Scarlet Pimpernel *(Anagallis arvensis*
    ssp. *arvensis)*
Sea Beet *(Beta vulgaris* ssp. *maritima)*
Sea Mayweed
    (Tripleurospermum maritimum)
Small Scabious *(Scabiosa columbaria)*
Spear Thistle *(Cirsium vulgare)*
Squinancywort *(Asperula cynanchica)*
Strawberry Clover
    (Trifolium fragiferum)

Tall Melilot *(Melilotus altissimus)*
Thrift, Sea Pink *(Armeria maritima)*
Tree-mallow *(Lavatera arborea)*
Viper's-bugloss *(Echium vulgare)*
White Stonecrop *(Sedum album)*
Wild Carrot
    (Daucus carota ssp. *carota)*
Wild Clary *(Salvia verbenaca)*
Wild Madder *(Rubia peregrina)*
Wild Marjoram *(Origanum vulgare)*
Wild Teasel *(Dipsacus fullonum)*
Wild Thyme *(Thymus polytrichus)*
Wood Sage *(Teucrium scorodonia)*
Yellow-rattle *(Rhinanthus minor)*
Yellow Vetchling *(Lathyrus aphaca)*
Yellow-wort *(Blackstonia perfoliata)*

Opposite: *Lesser Centaury*

Right: *View along the west coast of Portland towards Chesil Bank*

WALK 8

DORSET HEATH AND MARSH GENTIANS ON UNSPOILT DORSET HEATHLAND
Hartland Moor National Nature Reserve

A late summer walk on some of Dorset's best remaining heathland. Starting 3 miles (5 km) south-east of Wareham we first follow the path of an old clay tramway with a distant view of Corfe Castle. We then follow tracks across the moor, passing a flower-rich pond, before reaching a minor road on the far side of the moor near Hartland Stud.

We follow this road northwards with fine heathland views on both sides, before turning east and finally south-east and returning to our parking place along minor roads.

We see many heathland flowers on the moor including Dorset Heath, Dwarf Gorse, Marsh Gentian and the insectivorous Round-leaved Sundew. At the pond we also see flowers of wet places including Fen Bedstraw, Lesser Skullcap, Lesser Water-plantain, Marsh Pennywort and Square-stalked St. John's-wort.

Time of year:	late July to late August
Distance:	about 4½ miles (7 km)
Difficulty:	easy with no appreciable hills
Parking:	on roadside verge near track to Middlebere Farm at SY 963 854 (free)
Directions to parking area:	from Wareham take the A351 south towards Swanage. After 3¾ miles (6 km) turn left at a roundabout, signposted "Wych Farm Oil Field (works access)" and "Norden Park & Ride". Turn left after 50 yards (45 metres), signposted "Slepe 1½ Arne 3". Continue for 1¾ miles (2¾ km) until you see a track on your right with a sign to Middlebere Farm.
Ordnance Survey maps:	1:50,000 Landranger 195 Bournemouth & Purbeck 1:25,000 Explorer OL 15 Purbeck & South Dorset
Public transport:	none
Refreshments:	none (nearest on A351)
Toilets:	none

Walk 8

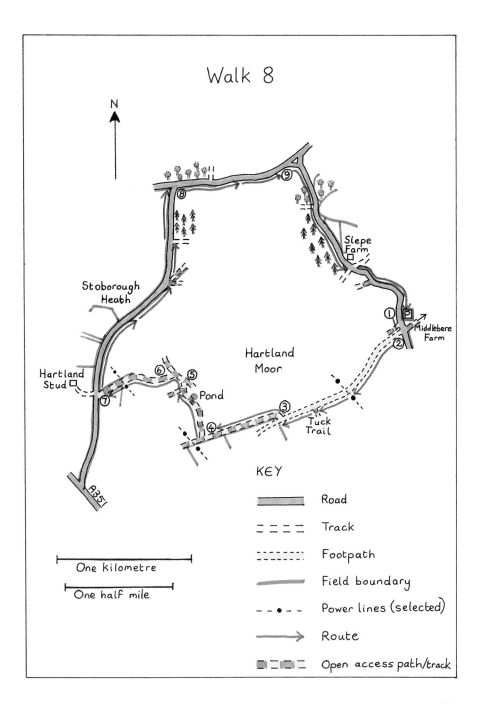

KEY

▬▬▬	Road
= = = =	Track
··········	Footpath
﹏﹏	Field boundary
– – •– –	Power lines (selected)
⟶	Route
▣▭▭▭	Open access path/track

One kilometre

One half mile

ROUTE

Warning: Please keep strictly to the route: there are dangerous bogs on the moor.

1.   Walk from where you have parked to a gate (waymarked "The National Trust" and "Hartland Way") on the west side of the road, opposite the track to Middlebere Farm.
     In the dry areas to the west of the road are Bell Heather, Dwarf Gorse and Heather, while in the wetter parts are Cross-leaved Heath, Dorset Heath, Marsh Gentian and the insectivorous Round-leaved Sundew.
2.   Go through the gate on to a footpath - the route of an old clay tramway - and follow it (roughly south-west) for ¾ mile (1¼ km) until you reach a narrow animal grid. Here a track goes off to the half right, while the footpath continues straight ahead over the animal grid. There is a distant view of Corfe Castle to the left (roughly south) from the tramway.
     Carline and Dwarf Thistles, Eyebright and Wild Thyme are found along the tramway, possibly resulting from the use of chalk or limestone hardcore for the track.

Marsh Gentian

When visiting Corfe Castle, P.D. James's Commander Dalgliesh

"...spent some time searching unsuccessfully for marsh gentians in the swampy scrubland..."

From *The Black Tower*, P.D.James

You should, however, have better luck on Hartland Moor! Although scarce and declining in Britain as a whole, Marsh Gentian retains strongholds round the Poole Basin. Found in Dorset in well-grazed wet heaths and at the edges of bogs, this beautiful flower seems strangely out of place in its surroundings.

The flowers are about 1 inch (2½ cm) across and 2 inches (5 cm) long; they are an intense blue with whitish spots inside and greenish stripes outside.

"...perhaps the best flower to take leave of the year with, if one were fortunate to find it, would be Marsh Gentian,...its tube is of so deep a blue, that as one gazes down, inches change to fathoms."

From *A Prospect of Flowers*, Andrew Young

Opposite: Marsh Gentian

3. Ignore the footpath straight ahead and bear right (roughly north-west) along the track, leaving the Hartland Way and path of the tramway. Follow the track (roughly west) for a further 700 yards (640 metres) until, shortly before it passes under power lines, you reach a junction with a track on your right at a post marked "English Nature" and "Water ⇨".

4. Turn right (roughly north) on to this track and follow it for 500 yards (460 metres), passing a small pond on your right, until you reach a track crossing ahead of you.
In and around the pond are Branched Bur-reed, Fen Bedstraw, Lesser Skullcap, Lesser Water-plantain, Marsh Pennywort, Marsh Speedwell, Saw-wort and Square-stalked St. John's-wort.

5. Turn left (roughly north-west) on to this track and follow it for 50 yards (45 metres) until it forks at a post marked "English Nature", "Water ⇨" and " ⇦ Water".

6. Take the left hand fork (roughly west) and follow it for 600 yards (550 metres), until you reach a gate at a road, almost opposite the entrance to Hartland Stud.
Dorset Heath is found beside the track shortly after the fork.

Opposite: *Heathland landscape at Hartland Moor*

Below: *Small flower-rich pond on Hartland Moor*

Heathland

"They were the mummied heath-bells of the past summer, originally tender and purple, now washed colourless by Michaelmas rains, and dried to dead skins by October suns. So low was an individual sound from these that a combination of hundreds only just emerged from silence ...each of the tiny trumpets was seized on, entered, scoured and emerged from by the wind as thoroughly as if it were as vast as a crater."

From *The Return of the Native*, Thomas Hardy

Hardy's powerful language evokes the character of Egdon heath - his name for the heathland in the east of Dorset, much diminished since his time by agriculture, building and forestry. The areas that do remain are rich in wildlife and Hartland Moor National Nature Reserve is a prime example. Heathland must be actively managed by cutting, burning or grazing to enable its typical assemblage of plants to triumph over unwanted invaders.

Besides the flowers you see as you cross the moor, on a sunny day you may also find butterflies such as Brimstone, Clouded Yellow, Common Blue, Gatekeeper, Grayling, Marbled White, Red Admiral, Small Copper and Small Heath; the beautiful Emperor Dragonfly can also sometimes be spotted close to water. You may also be lucky enough to see the rare Dartford Warbler - possibly as a fleeting glimpse of a small dark bird flying into the cover of a gorse bush.

7. Go through the gate and turn right (roughly north) on to the road. Follow the road (generally north or north-east) for 1 mile (about 1½ km) until you reach a junction. There are good heathland views to both sides of the road.
Devil's-bit Scabious and Yellow Bartsia can be seen on the left hand verge.

8. Turn right (east) at the junction and follow the road for ½ mile (800 metres) until you reach a junction with a road on your right.

9. Turn right (roughly east) at the junction (signposted "Corfe Castle 3") and follow the winding road (generally south-east), taking special care of the traffic, for just over a mile (1¾ km) until you reach your car.
The insectivorous Pale Butterwort is found in a ditch to the right of the road shortly after the junction.

Top right: *Devil's-bit Scabious*

Bottom right: *Yellow Bartsia*

Opposite: *Banks of Dwarf Gorse and Bell Heather*

Dorset Heath

Dorset Heath is perhaps *the* Dorset flower and was our winner of Plantlife's County Flower competition.

It is a nationally rare plant, mainly confined in Britain to parts of Dorset and Cornwall. In Dorset itself it is restricted to wet heathland in a small area around the Poole Basin.

Dorset Heath is a shrubby plant with spikes of striking reddish pink tubular flowers about ⅜ inch (1 cm) long. The leaves are small and arranged in whorls of 3, or sometimes 4, around the stem.

It often hybridises with another much more common plant found in similar places, Cross-leaved Heath. This has smaller, more globular, pink flowers in a distinct head and leaves in cross-shaped whorls of 4 around the stem. The hybrids have some of the characteristics of both parents and are common on Hartland Moor.

The most reliable way to distinguish the true Dorset Heath from the hybrid is to examine the tips of the stamens inside the flowers. The hybrid has two small appendages beneath the tip while the Dorset Heath has no appendages. The drawings below illustrate this difference:

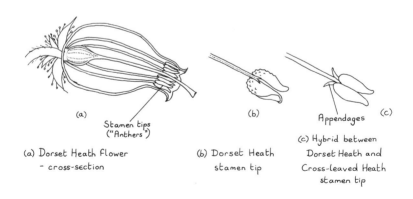

(a)
Stamen tips
("Anthers")

(a) Dorset Heath Flower
- cross-section

(b)

(b) Dorset Heath
stamen tip

Appendages   (c)

(c) Hybrid between
Dorset Heath and
Cross-leaved Heath
stamen tip

Opposite: Dorset Heath

Some of the flowers you may see on this walk

Agrimony *(Agrimonia eupatoria)*
Bell Heather *(Erica cinerea)*
Betony *(Stachys officinalis)*
Bittersweet, Woody Nightshade
    (Solanum dulcamara)
Bog Asphodel *(Narthecium ossifragum)*
Branched Bur-reed
    (Sparganium erectum)
Broad-leaved Willowherb
    (Epilobium montanum)
Buck's-horn Plantain
    (Plantago coronopus)
Carline Thistle *(Carlina vulgaris)*
Common Bird's-foot-trefoil, Eggs-and-
    Bacon *(Lotus corniculatus)*
Common Centaury
    (Centaurium erythraea)
Common Fleabane
    (Pulicaria dysenterica)
Common Knapweed, Hardheads
    (Centaurea nigra)
Common Ragwort *(Senecio jacobaea)*
Common Restharrow *(Ononis repens)*
Common Stork's-bill
    (Erodium cicutarium)
Cross-leaved Heath *(Erica tetralix)*
Devil's-bit Scabious *(Succisa pratensis)*
Dodder *(Cuscuta epithymum)*
Dorset Heath *(Erica ciliaris)*
Dwarf Gorse *(Ulex minor)*
Dwarf Thistle, Stemless Thistle
    (Cirsium acaule)
Enchanter's-nightshade
    (Circaea lutetiana)
Eyebright *(Euphrasia officinalis agg.)*
Fen Bedstraw *(Galium uliginosum)*
Fairy Flax *(Linum catharticum)*
Greater Bird's-foot-trefoil
    (Lotus pedunculatus)

Hare's-foot Clover *(Trifolium arvense)*
Heather *(Calluna vulgaris)*
Heath Milkwort
    (Polygala serpyllifolia)
Hemp-agrimony
    (Eupatorium cannabinum)
Herb-Robert *(Geranium robertianum)*
Lady's Bedstraw *(Galium verum)*
Lesser Skullcap *(Scutellaria minor)*
Lesser Spearwort
    (Ranunculus flammula)
Lesser Stitchwort *(Stellaria graminea)*
Lesser Water-plantain
    (Baldellia ranunculoides)
Marsh Gentian
    (Gentiana pneumonanthe)
Marsh Pennywort
    (Hydrocotyle vulgaris)
Marsh Speedwell *(Veronica scutellata)*
Marsh Thistle *(Cirsium palustre)*
Marsh Willowherb
    (Epilobium palustre)
Meadowsweet *(Filipendula ulmaria)*
Mouse-ear-hawkweed
    (Pilosella officinarum)
Nipplewort *(Lapsana communis)*
Oxeye Daisy *(Leucanthemum vulgare)*
Pale Butterwort *(Pinguicula lusitanica)*
Pale Flax *(Linum bienne)*
Perforate St. John's-wort
    (Hypericum perforatum)
Purple-loosestrife *(Lythrum salicaria)*
Red Bartsia *(Odontites vernus)*
Red Clover *(Trifolium pratense)*
Redshank *(Persicaria maculosa)*
Ribwort Plantain *(Plantago lanceolata)*
Round-leaved Sundew
    (Drosera rotundifolia)
Sand Spurrey *(Spergularia rubra)*

Saw-wort *(Serratula tinctoria)*
Scarlet Pimpernel *(Anagallis arvensis*
    ssp. *arvensis)*
Selfheal *(Prunella vulgaris)*
Sheep's-bit *(Jasione montana)*
Sheep's Sorrel *(Rumex acetosella)*
Silverweed *(Potentilla anserina)*
Spear Thistle *(Cirsium vulgare)*
Square-stalked St. John's-wort
    (Hypericum tetrapterum)
Thyme-leaved Speedwell
    (Veronica serpyllifolia)
Tormentil *(Potentilla erecta)*
Trailing St. John's-wort
    (Hypericum humifusum)

Tufted Vetch *(Vicia cracca)*
Vervain *(Verbena officinalis)*
Western Gorse *(Ulex gallii)*
White Clover *(Trifolium repens)*
Wild Carrot *(Daucus carota* ssp.
    carota)
Wild Parsnip *(Pastinaca sativa* var.
    sativa)
Wild Thyme *(Thymus polytrichus)*
Wood Sage *(Teucrium scorodonia)*
Yarrow *(Achillea millefolium)*
Yellow Bartsia
    (Parentucellia viscosa)

Overleaf: *Cowslip*
Below: *Dwarf Gorse and Bell Heather*

"Home, thank God, but like to fall
    O'er the threshold of the door;
I can hardly walk at all,
    And could not a half-mile more.
Oh! how weary are my feet!
And I'm spent with dust and heat.
Bit of meat? No; give me first
Just some tea to quench my thirst.
No; not wine - e'er so fine.
No; not gold - heap'd untold;
    But a cup or two of tea."

From *Goody Tired*,
William Barnes

BIBLIOGRAPHY

ALLSOP, K. (1972) *In the Country.* Hamish Hamilton.

ASHDOWN, D. (1996) *An Introduction to William Barnes, The Dorset Poet.* Dorset Books. Reprinted (1999).

BATH, F.R.L. (1977) *Flowers of William Barnes.* Friary Press Ltd.

BLAMEY, M., FITTER, R., FITTER, A. (2003) *Wild Flowers of Britain & Ireland.* A. & C. Black Publishers Ltd.

BLAMEY, M., GREY-WILSON, C. (1989) *The Illustrated Flora of Britain and Northern Europe.* Hodder and Stoughton.

BOWEN, H.J.M. (2000) *The Flora of Dorset.* Pisces Publications.

BRUNSDEN, D., Ed. (2003) *The Official Guide to the Jurassic Coast.* Coastal Publishing.

BURTON, A. (1999) *Recreational Path Guide, The Wessex Ridgeway.* Aurum Press Ltd. in association with the Ordnance Survey.

CRAMB, P. & M. (2003) *Wild Flowers of the Dorset Coast Path.* P. & M. Cramb.

DORSET WILDLIFE TRUST (1997) *The Natural History of Dorset.* The Dovecote Press Ltd.

DRAPER, J. (1986) *Dorset, The Complete Guide.* The Dovecote Press Ltd. Revised Ed. (1996).

DRAPER, J. & CHAPLIN, C. (1997) *Walking Dorset History.* The Dovecote Press Ltd.

EDWARDS, B., PEARMAN, D.A. (2004) *Dorset Rare Plant Register.* Dorset Environmental Records Centre in conjunction with the Botanical Society of the British Isles.

ENDECOTT, V. (2002) *The Dorset Days of Enid Blyton.* Ginger Pop Promotions.

FOLEY, M., CLARKE, S. (2005) *Orchids of the British Isles.* Griffin Press Publishing Ltd.

GOOD, R.D. (1948) *A Geographical Handbook of the Dorset Flora.* Dorset Natural History and Archaeological Society.

GRIFFITHS, E. (2003) *The Original Stour Valley Path.* Green Fields Books.

HARMAN, C., Ed. (1994) *The Diaries of Sylvia Townsend Warner.* Chatto & Windus Ltd.

HAWKINS, D. (1983) *Hardy's Wessex.* Macmillan London Ltd.

HAWKINS, D., Ed. (1996) *Dorset Bedside Book: A Collection of Prose and Poetry.* The Dovecote Press Ltd.

HORSFALL, A. (1991) *Names of Wild Flowers in Dorset.* A. Horsfall.

HYLAND, P. (1998) *Isle of Purbeck.* The Dovecote Press Ltd.

JENKINSON, M.N. (1991) *Wild Orchids of Dorset.* Orchid Sundries Ltd.